Math

Counting 1–10

Help the ant get to the sugar.
Color the numbers in order. Start with **1**.

	1	2	5	7
4	9	3	10	8
2	5	4	1	3
9	6	7	8	4
7	2	3	9	10

Counting Zero

Trace and write.

Count the cookies on the plates.
Write the number.

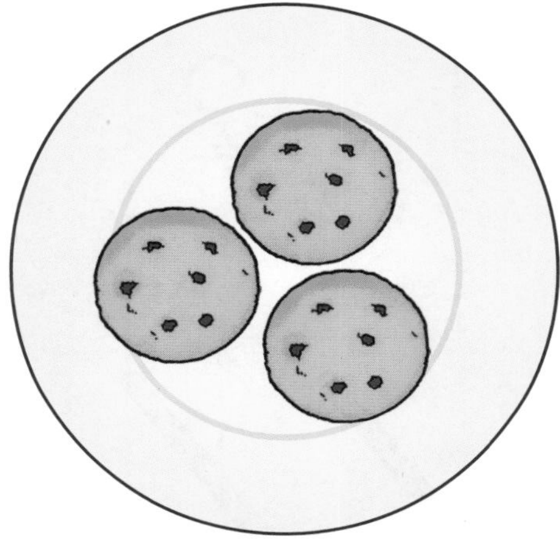

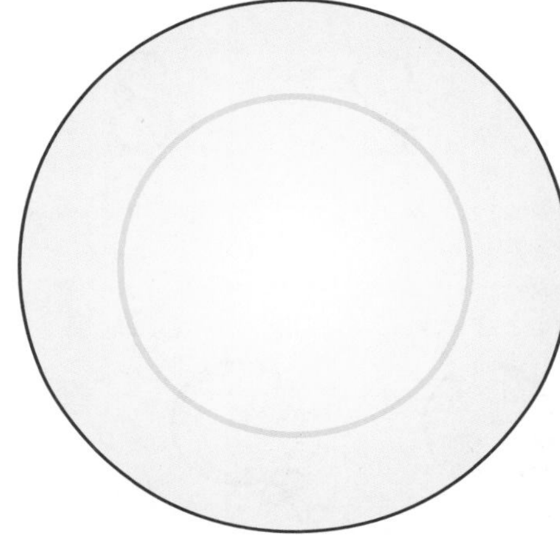

____ cookies ____ cookies

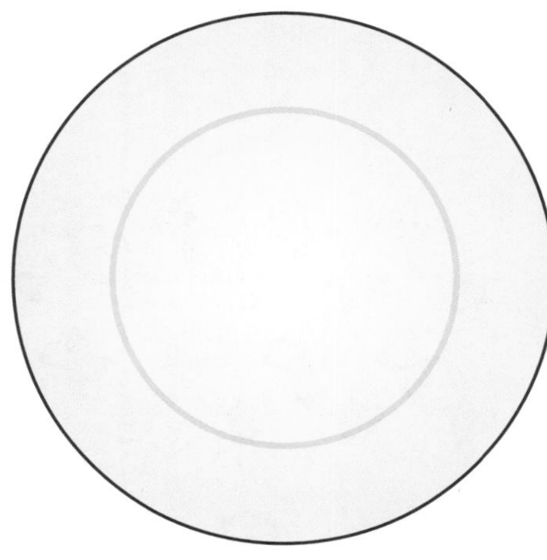

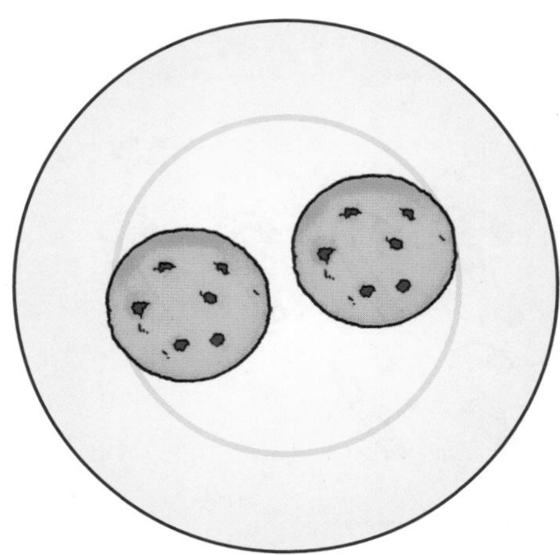

____ cookies ____ cookies

Counting 1–10

Count the candy.
Circle the number.

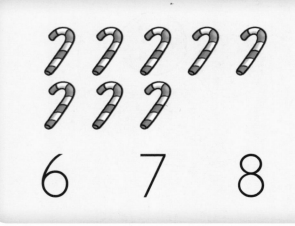

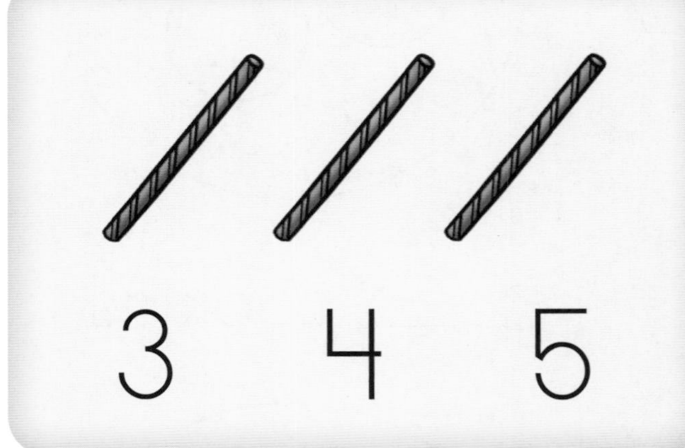

6 7 8

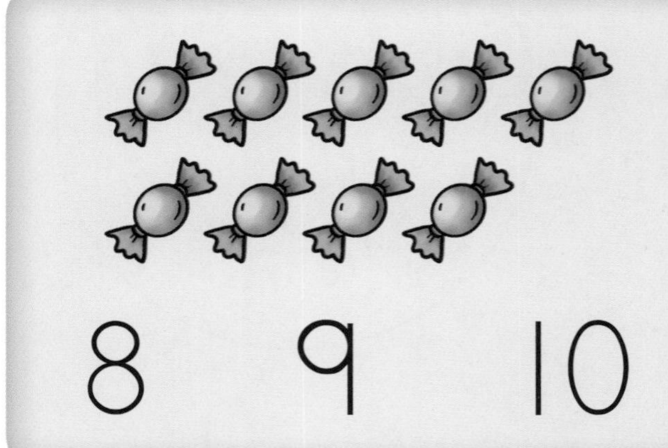

Draw **1** more.
Write how many in all.

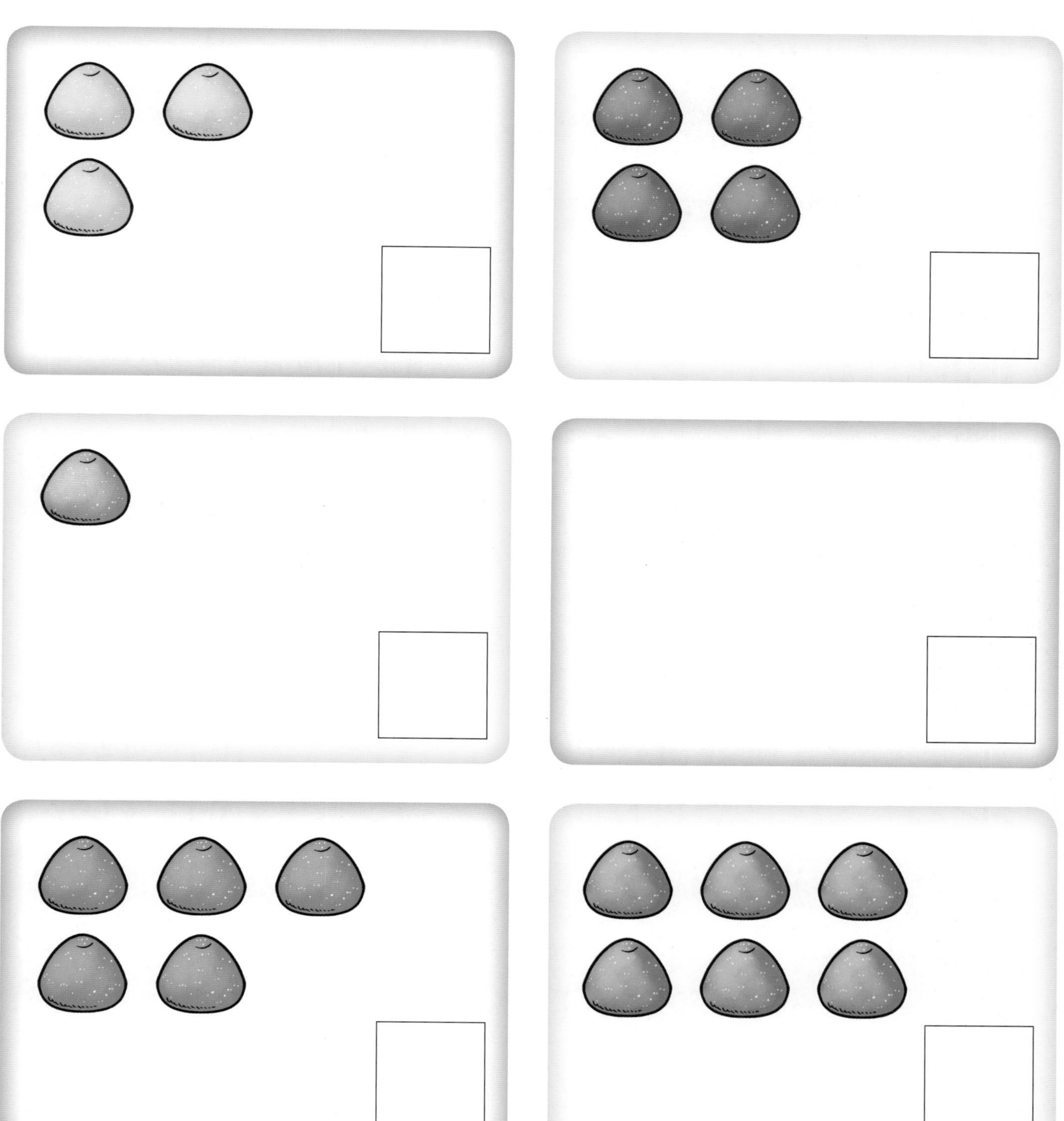

Counting 0–10

Color the cupcakes.

0 red   2 yellow
4 pink   6 brown

Help Max get to the doughnuts.
Write the missing numbers.

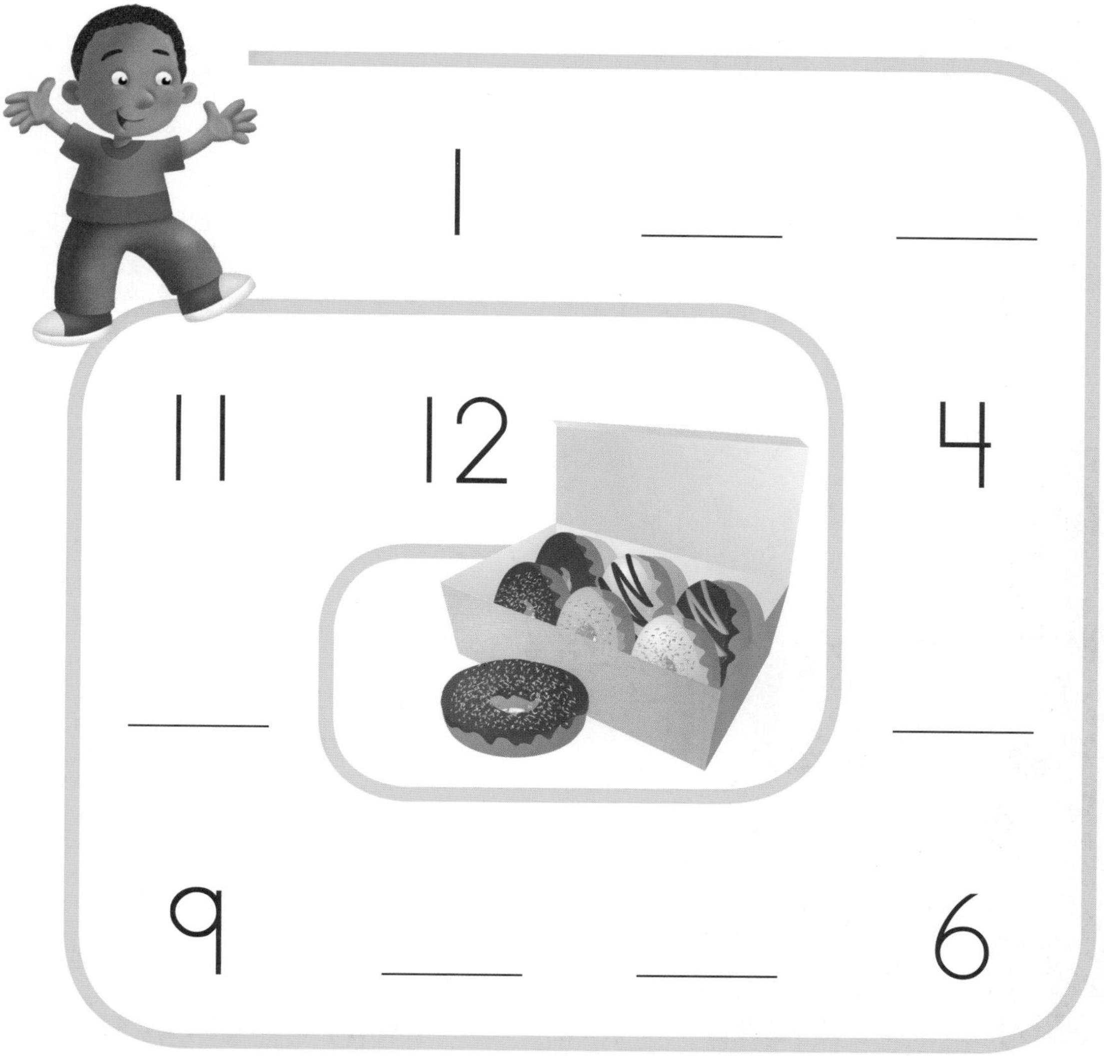

1 ___ ___

11 12 4

___ ___

9 ___ ___ 6

12 is 1 dozen. Draw an **X** on 1 dozen doughnuts.

Counting 1–12

Connect the dots.
Start with **1**.
Color it **red** and **green**.

Patterning

Color the last gumdrop in each column.
Follow the pattern.

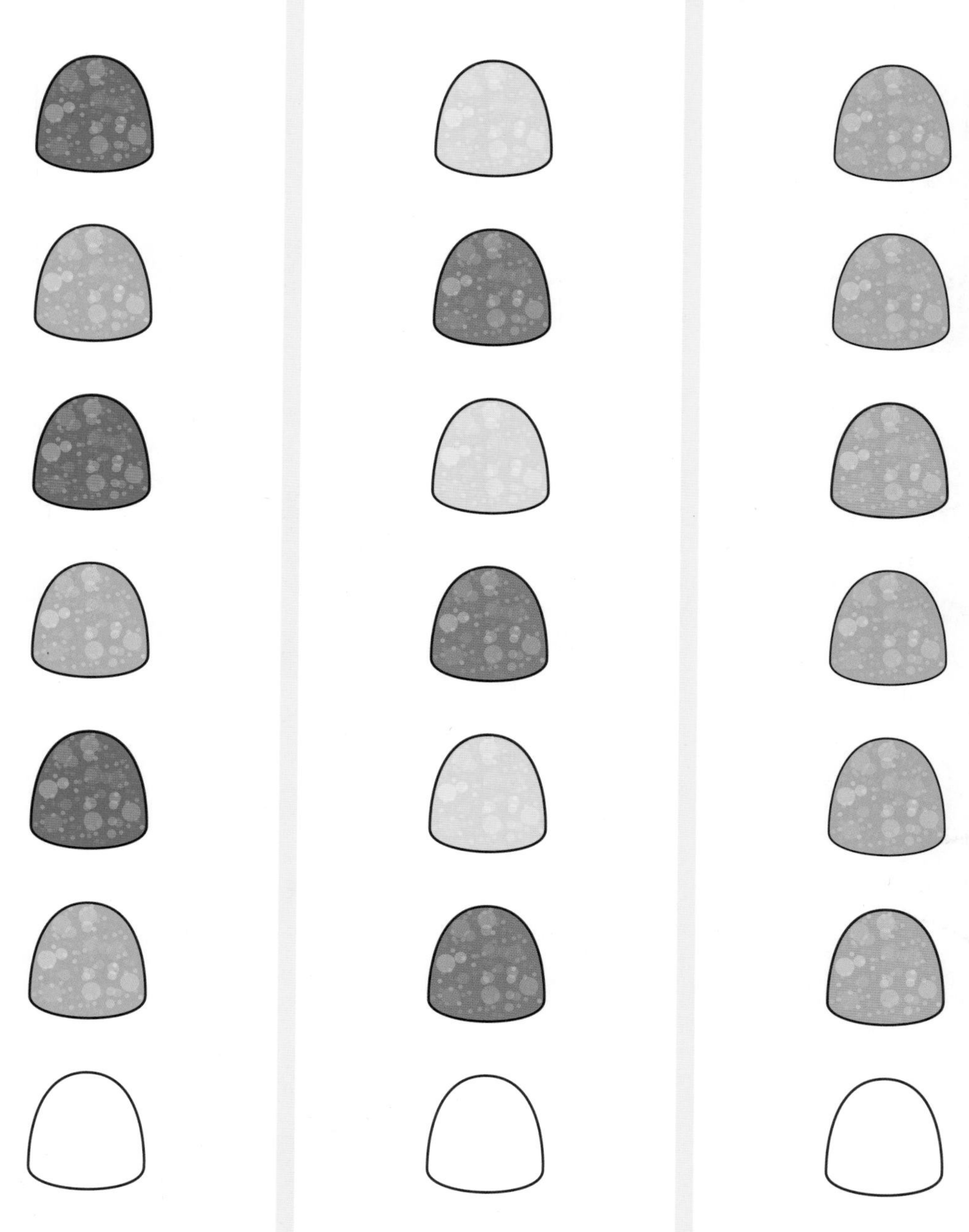

Money

Match.

5¢

4¢

3¢

6¢

Draw a line to make a match.

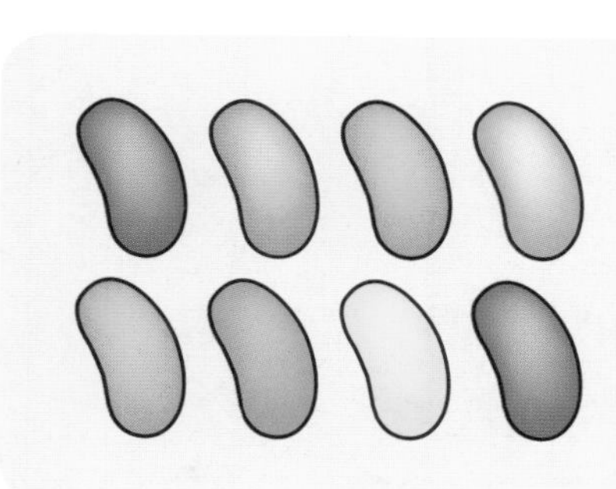

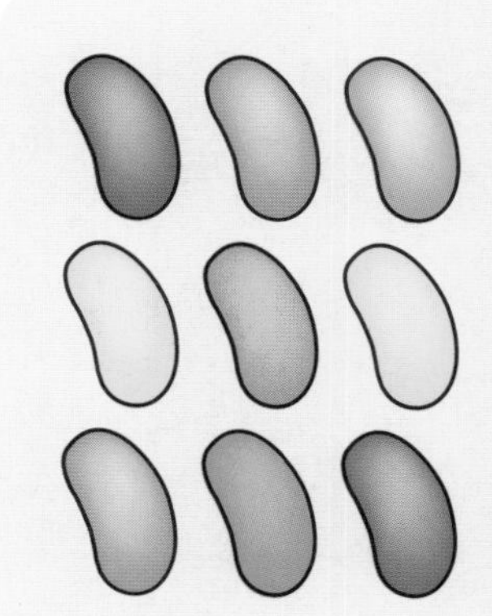

7

8

9

10

11

12

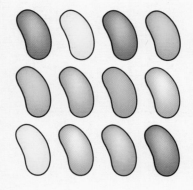

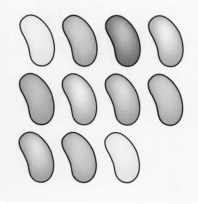

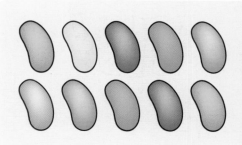

Numbers to 12

Write the letter for each number to find the sweet treat.

7 = a	8 = c	9 = e
10 = k	11 = p	12 = u

8	12	11	8	7	10	9
c						

Put an **X** on the sweet treat you found.

Counting 1–20

1	2	3	4	5	6	7	8	9	10
11	12	13	14	15	16	17	18	19	20

Trace the numbers. Write the missing numbers.

1 _____ _____ _____ 5

6 _____ _____ _____ 10

11 _____ _____ _____ 15

16 _____ _____ _____ 20

Draw **20** cookies.

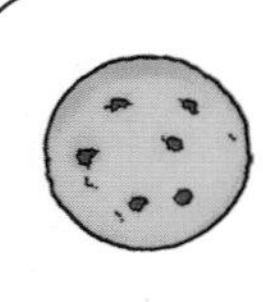

Counting 1–20

Put an **X** on the candy to show the amount.

X on 12

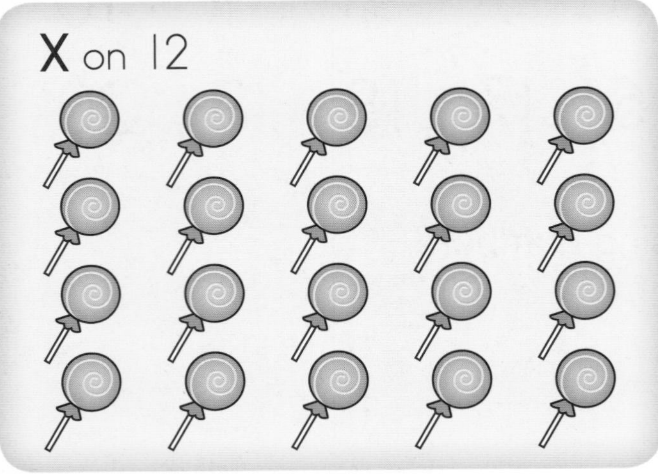

X on 18

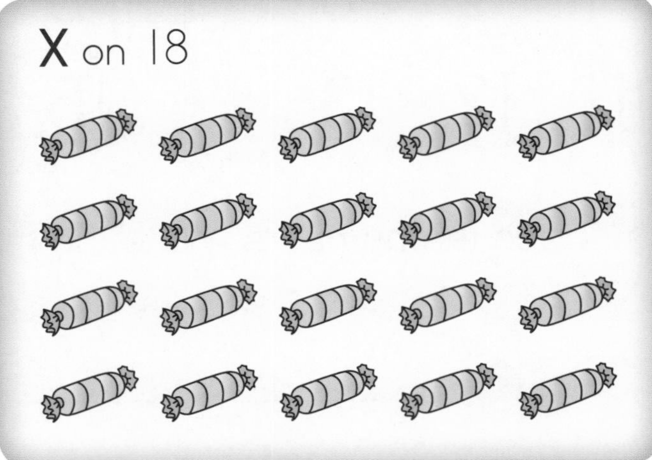

X on 20

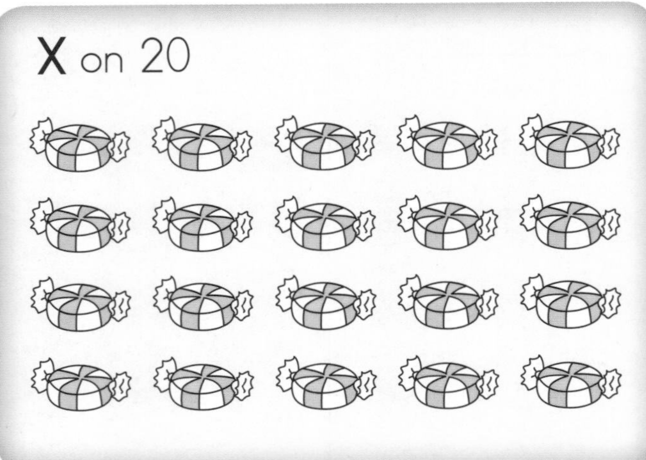

X on 17

X on 11

X on 16

Connect the dots.
Start with **1**.

10 9 11 8 12 7 13 6 14 5 15 4 16 3 17 2 18 1 20 19

Draw the cookie you like best in the jar.

Counting 1–25

Help Josh get to the bakery. Write the missing numbers. Count to **25**.

1 2 ____ ____

5

____ 9 8 ____ ____

____ 12 13 ____ ____

16

____ ____ ____ 17

21

22 ____ ____ 25

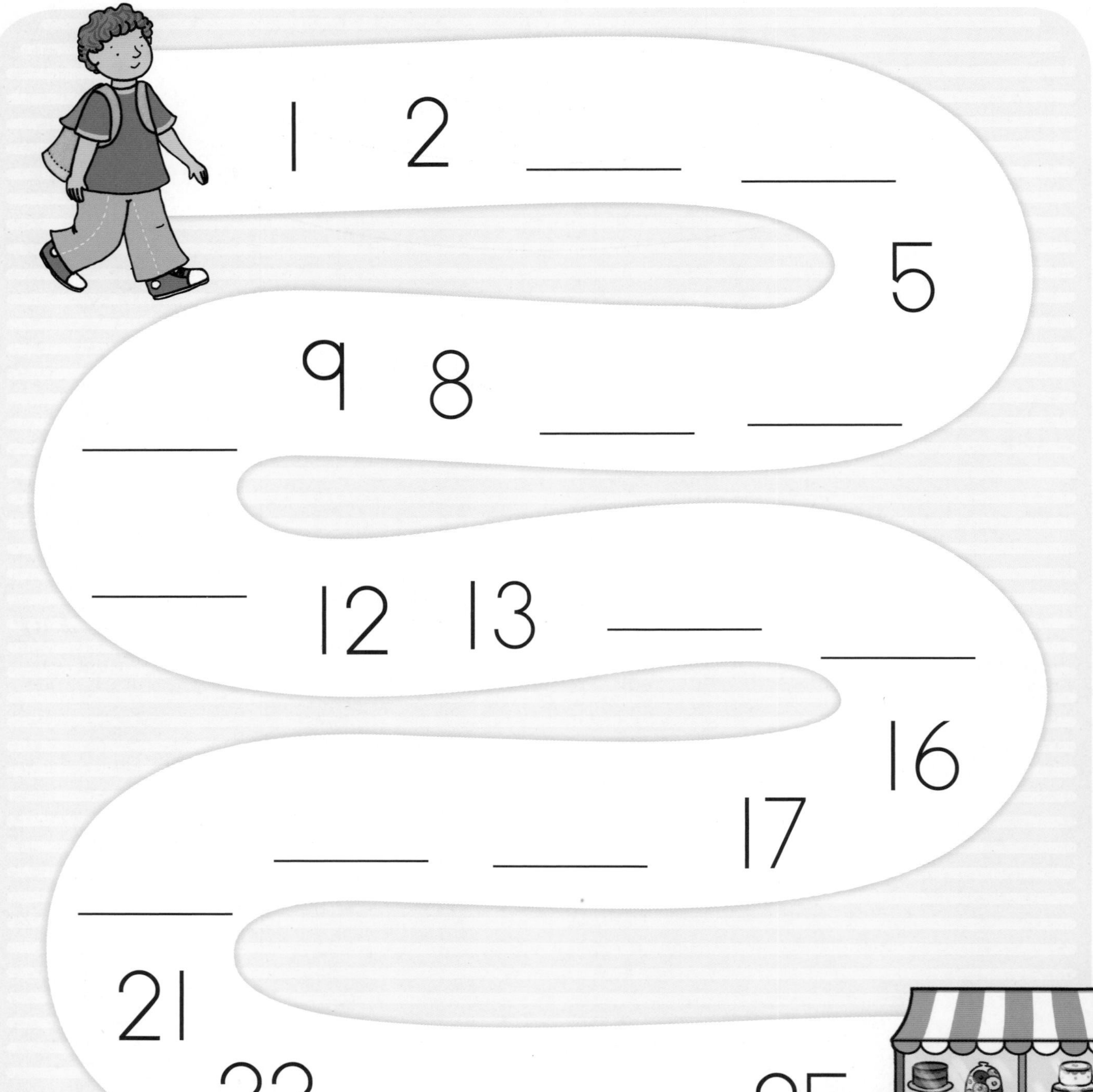

Counting 1–25

Connect the dots.
Start with **1**.

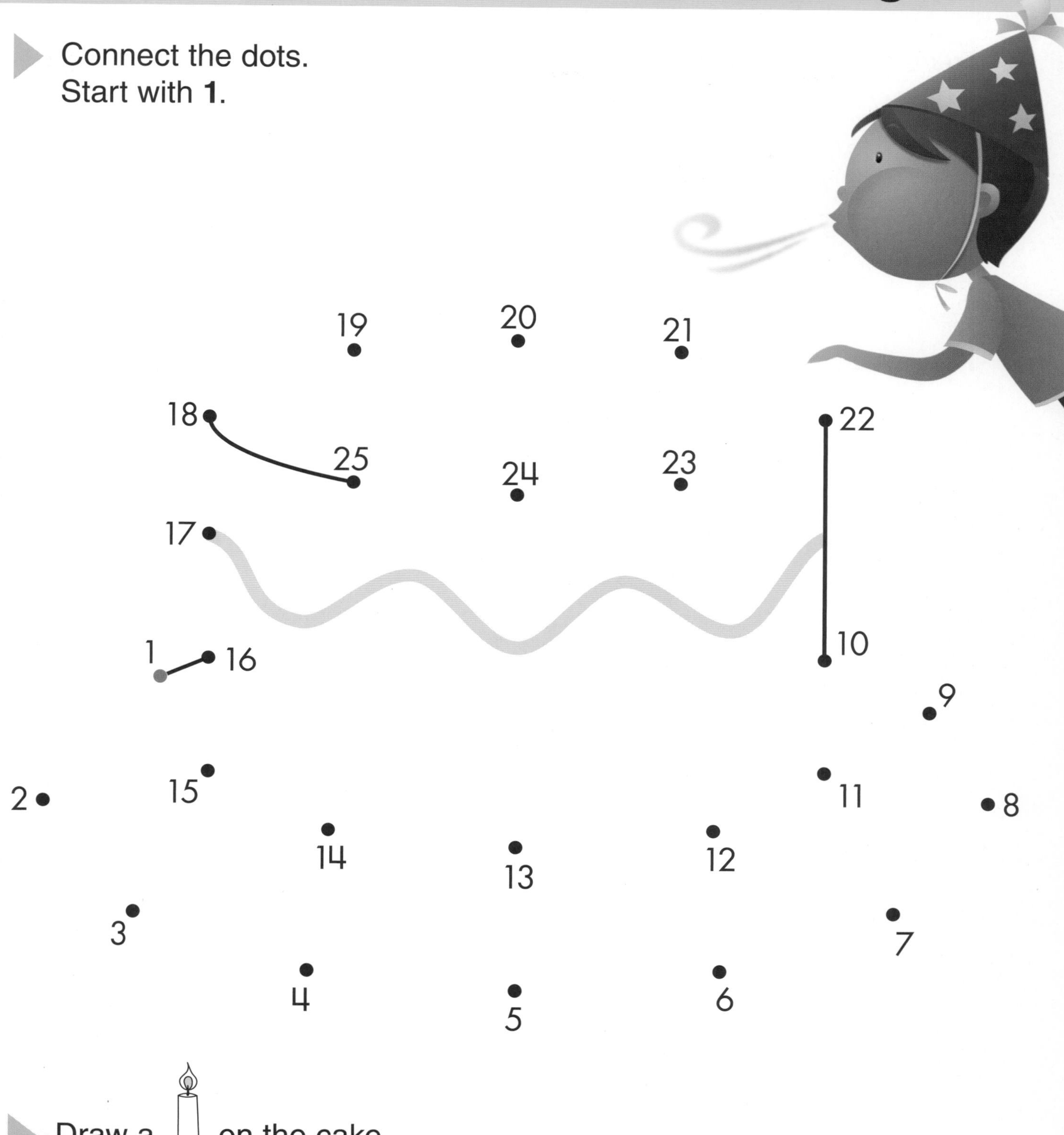

Draw a [candle] on the cake.

Shapes

Trace the shape of each snack. Color.

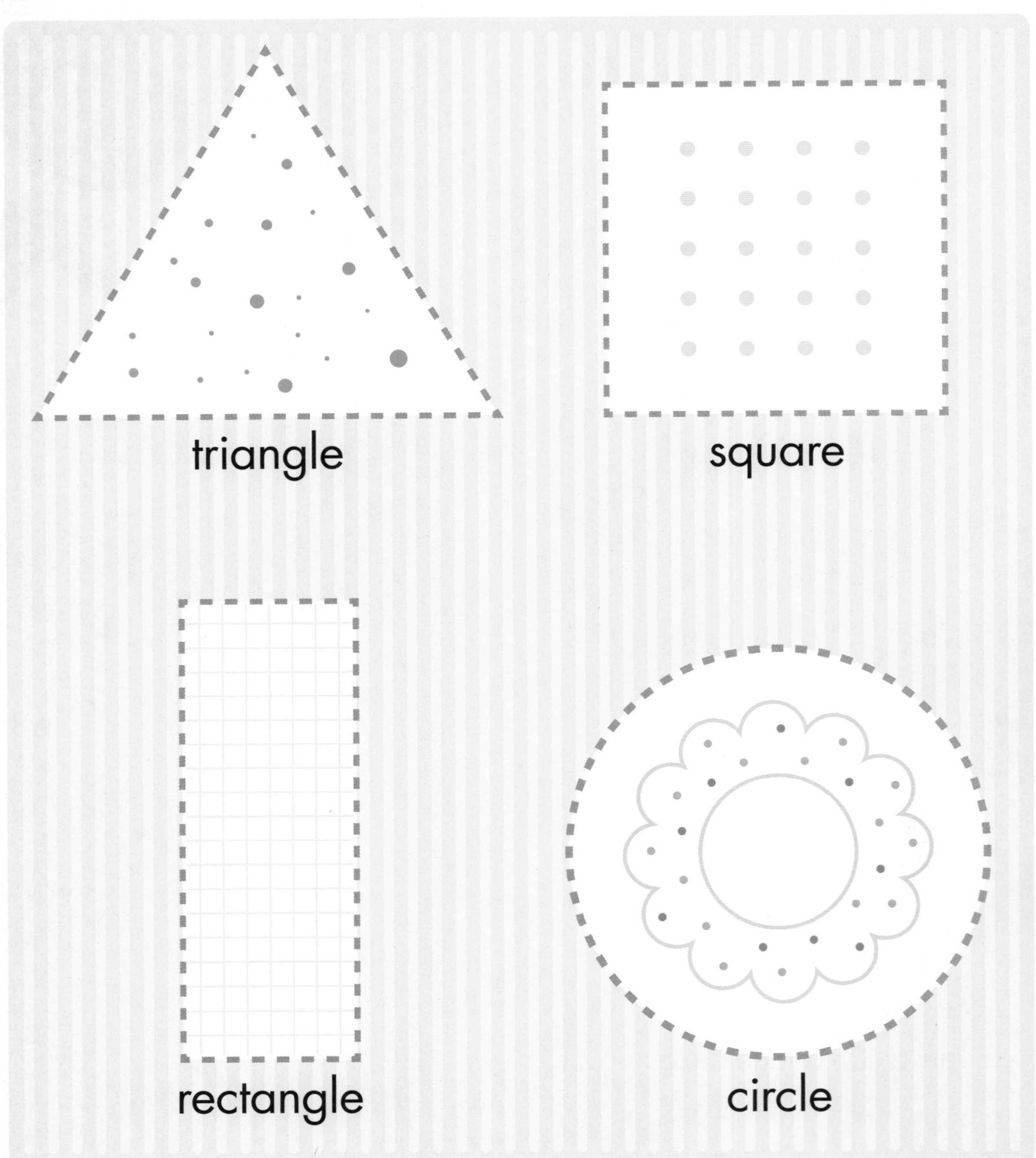

Draw the shapes.
Follow the pattern.

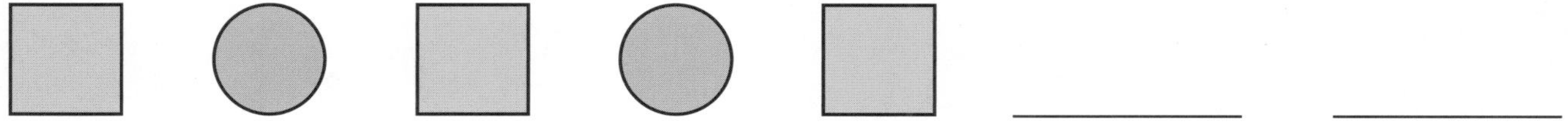

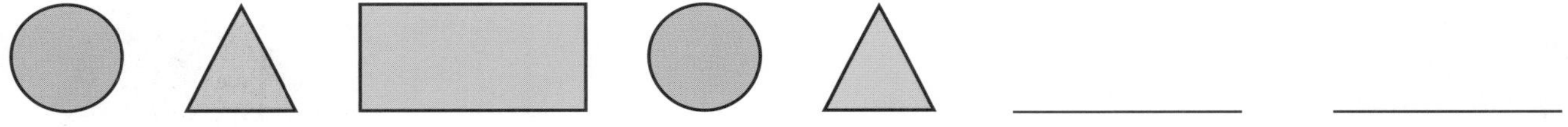

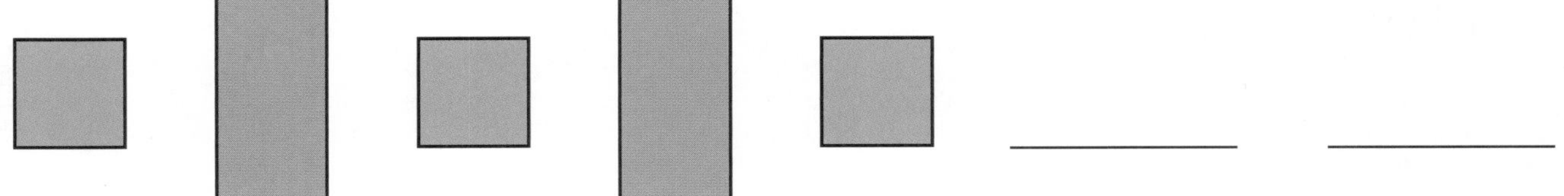

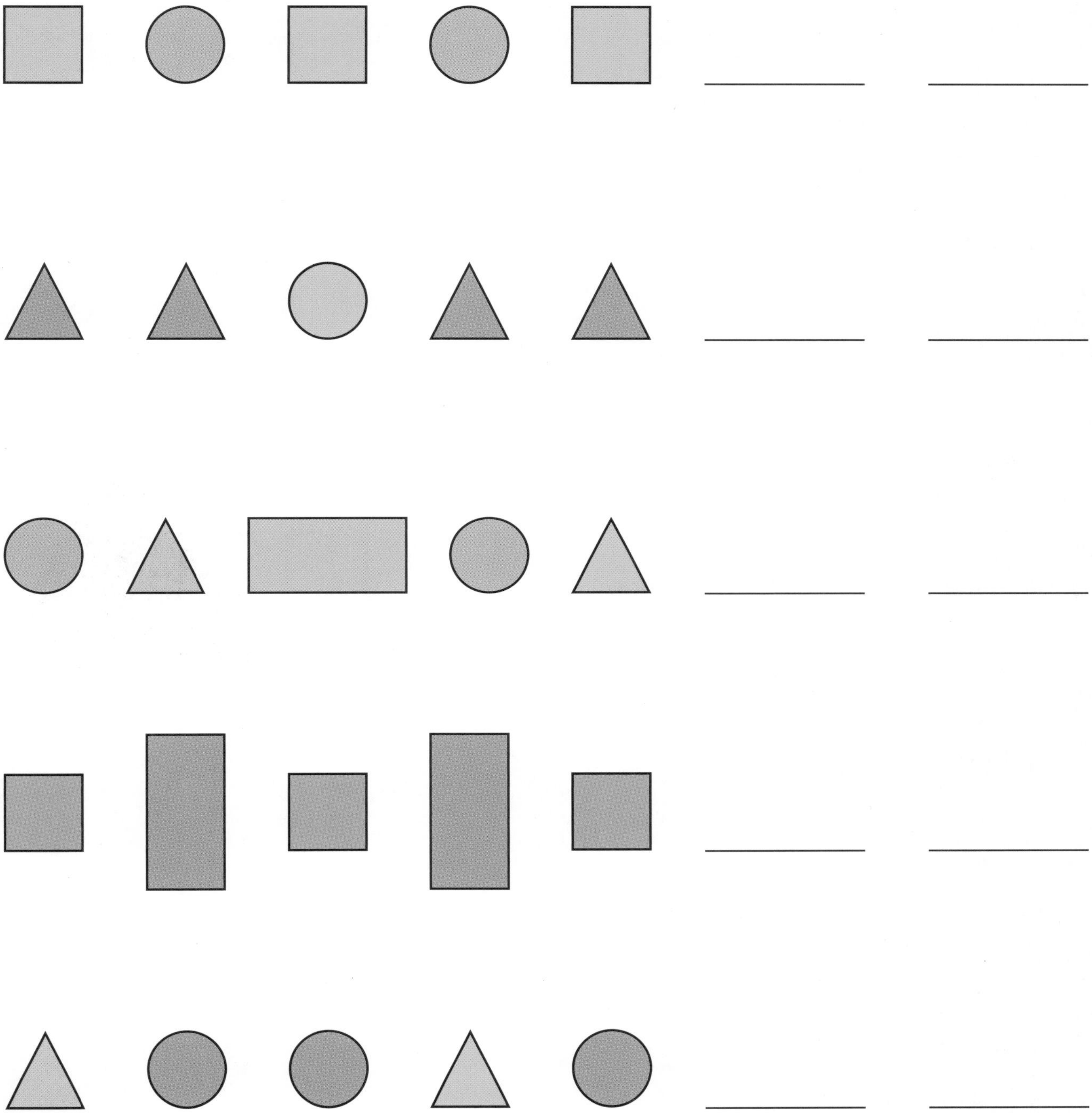

Draw a line to make a match.

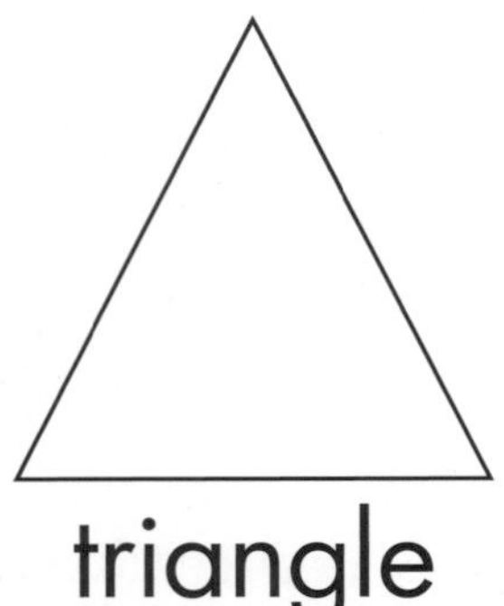

triangle

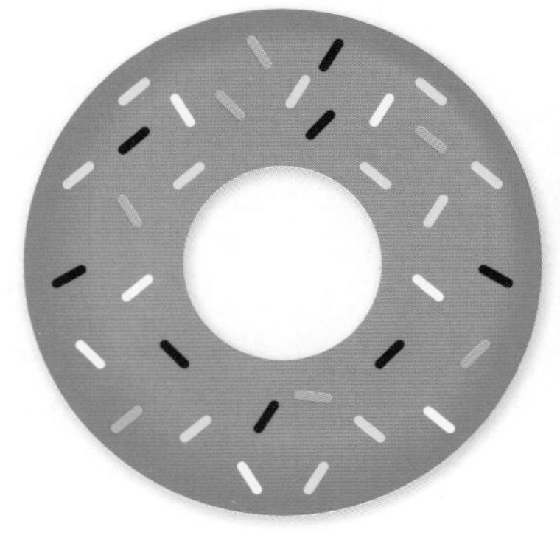

square

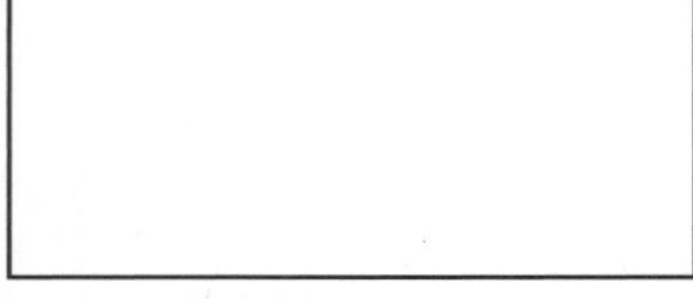

rectangle

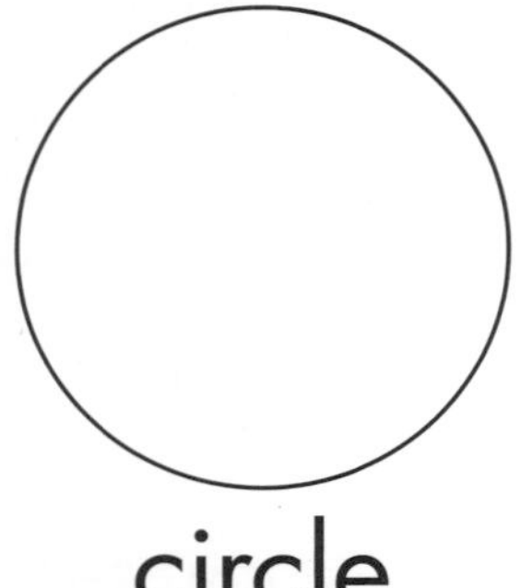

circle

Find the shapes. Color them.

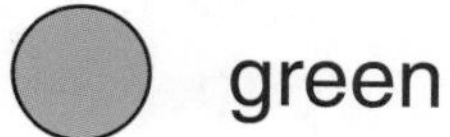
green

blue

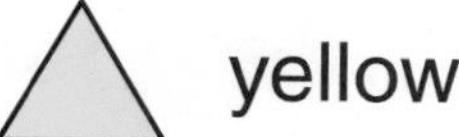
yellow

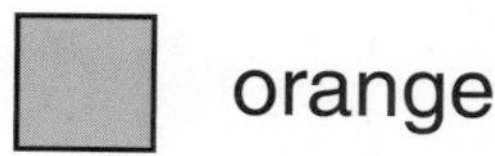
orange

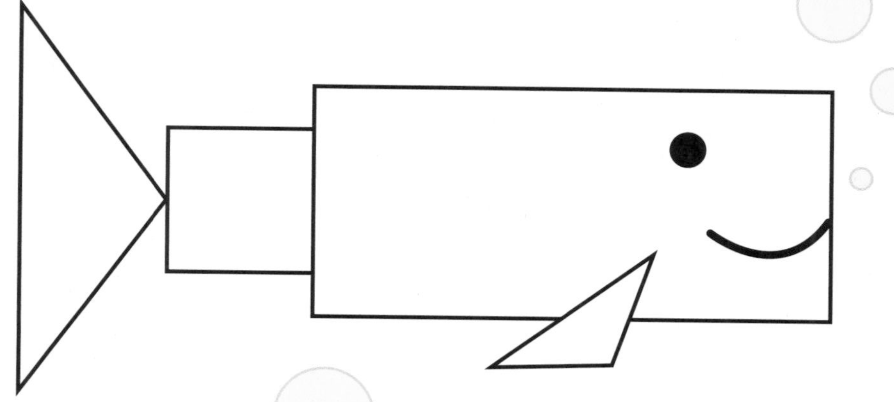

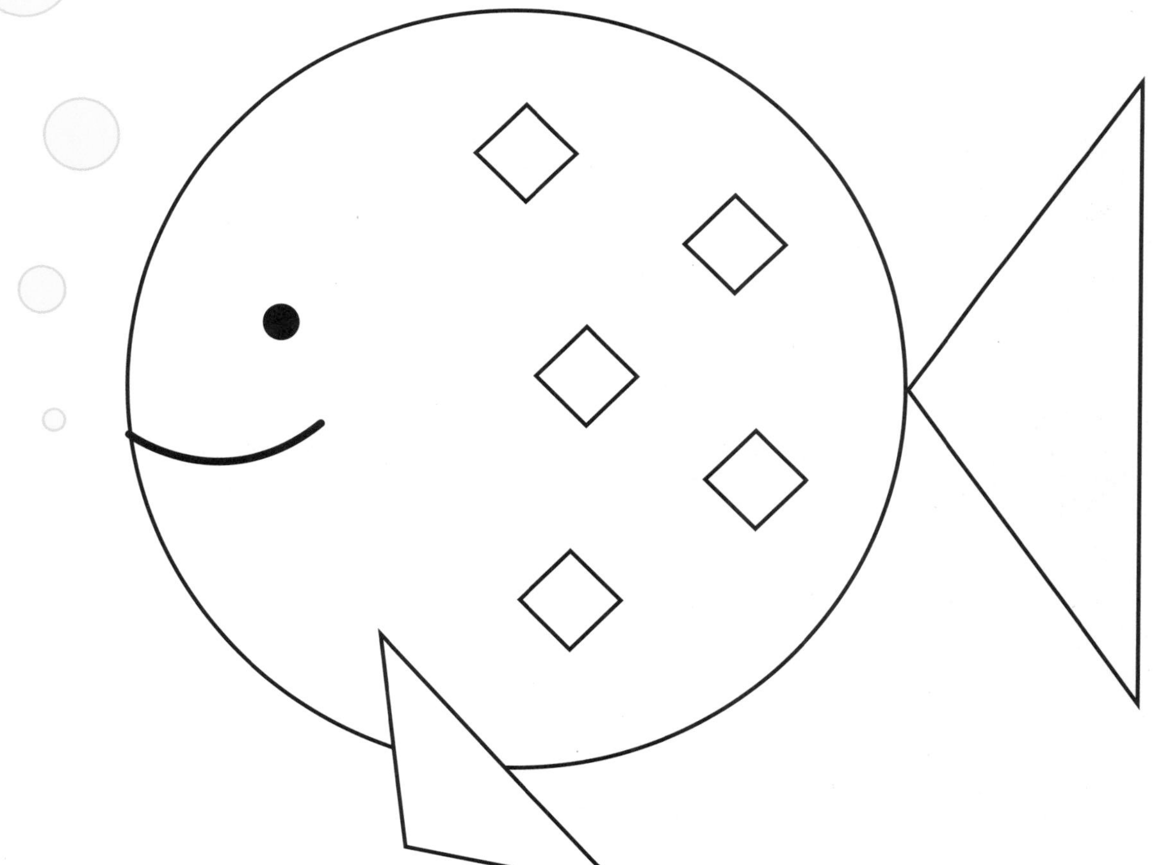

Patterning

Put an **X** on what comes next.
Follow the pattern.

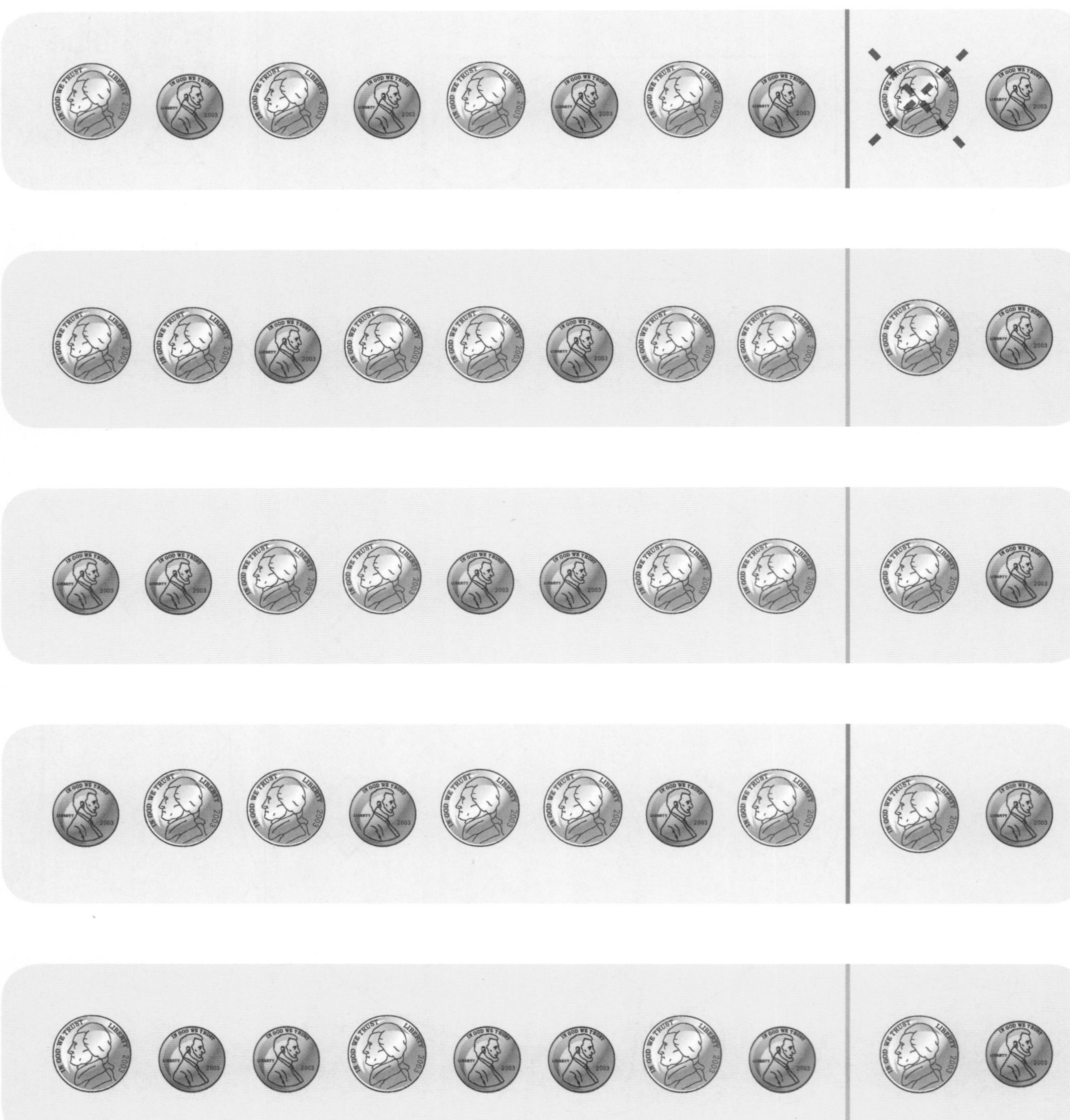

Counting by 5

Trace. Count by 5.

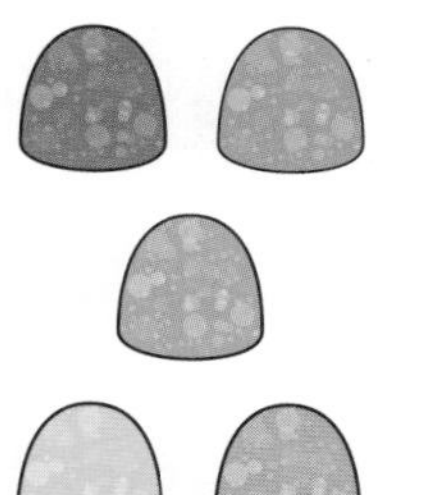
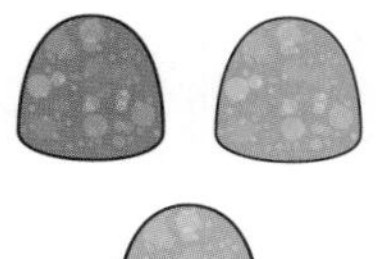
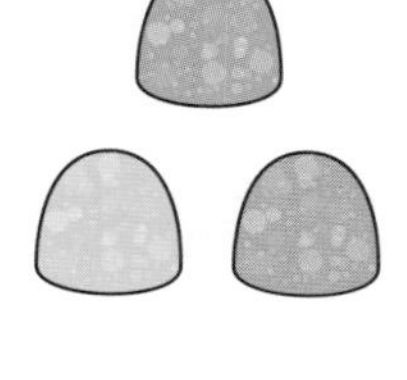
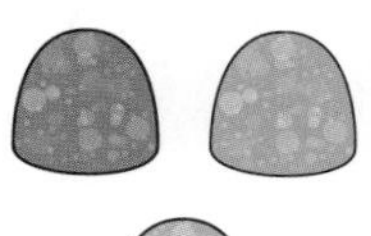
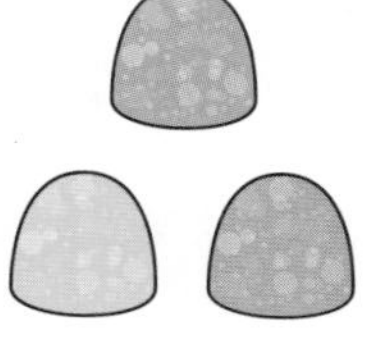
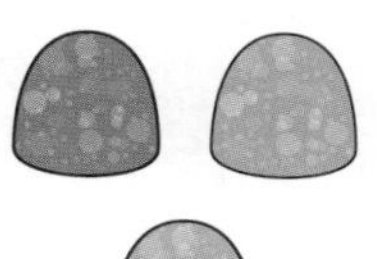
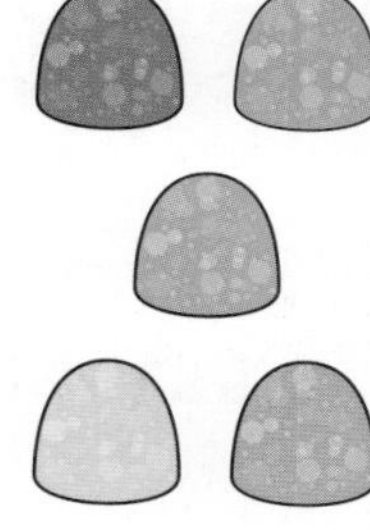

5 10 15 20 25

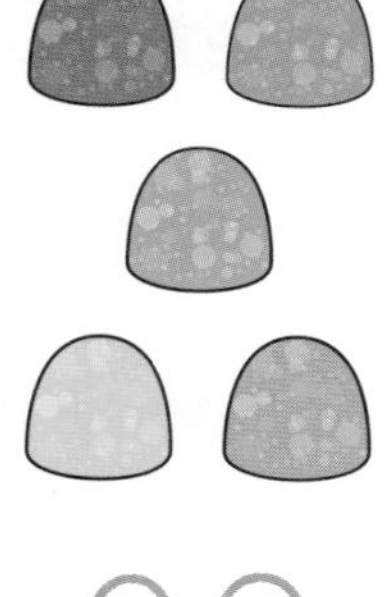
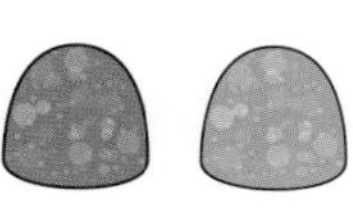
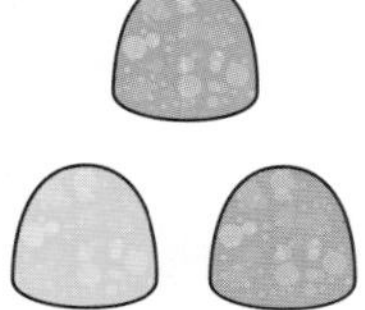
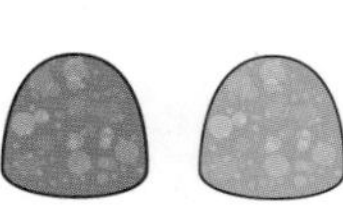
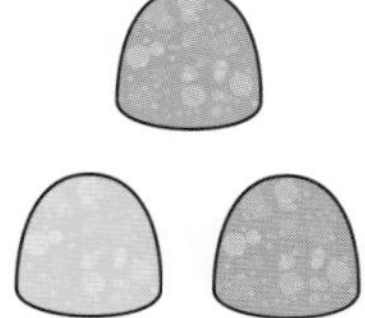
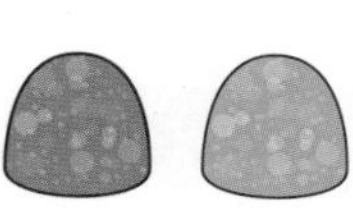
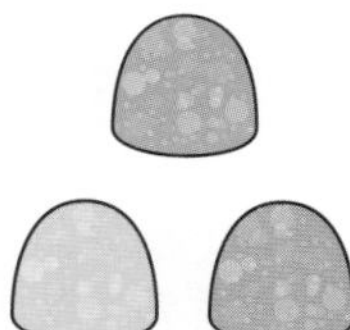
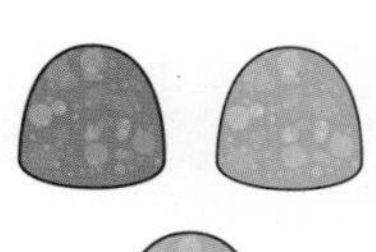
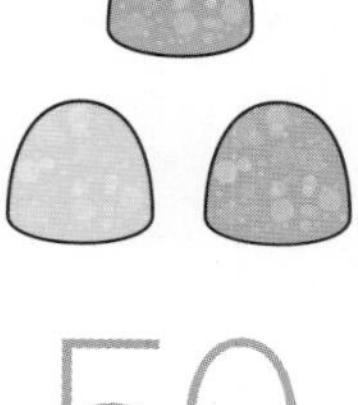

30 35 40 45 50

Write the missing numbers.

5 10 ____ ____ 25

30 ____ ____ 45 50

Counting by 5

5 10 15 20 25 30 35 40 45 50

Connect the dots to make a cookie.
Start with **5**.

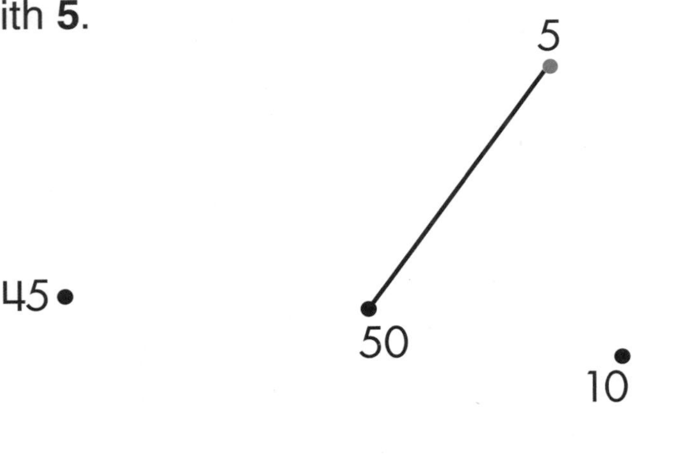

What shape is the cookie? Make an **X**.

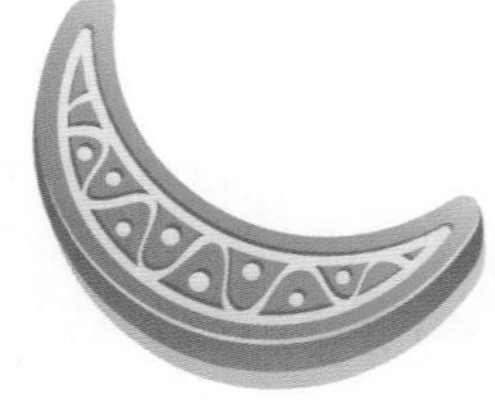

Make a Graph

Color one box for each sweet treat.

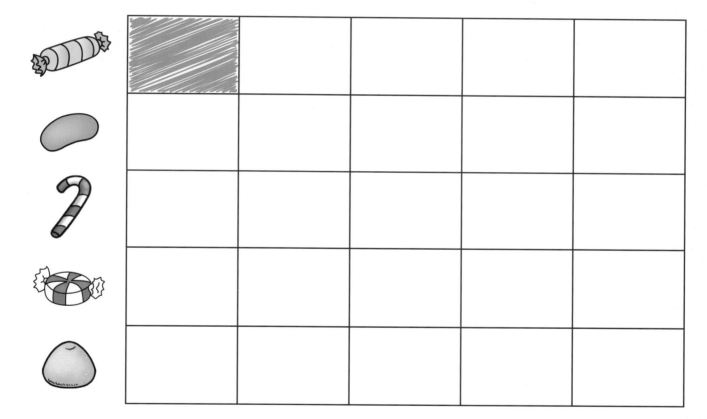

X the most.

  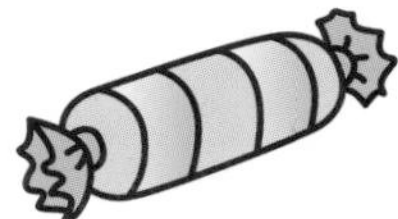  

Counting by 10

 I penny is I cent.

 I dime is 10 cents.

 = 

▶ Trace the numbers.

10 cents

20 cents

30 cents

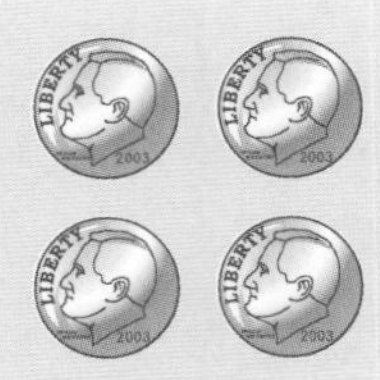

40 cents

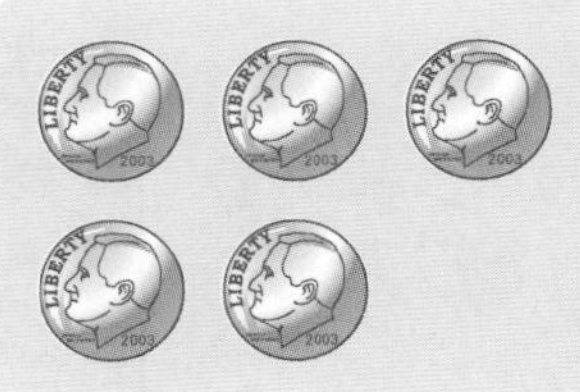

50 cents

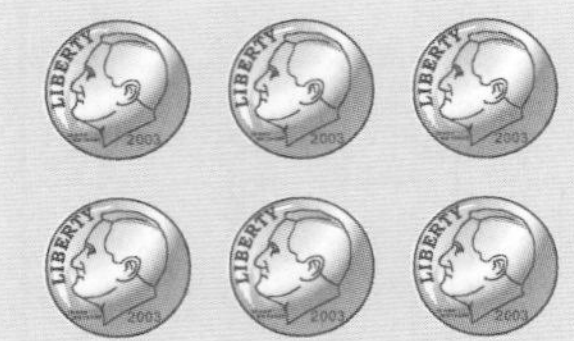

60 cents

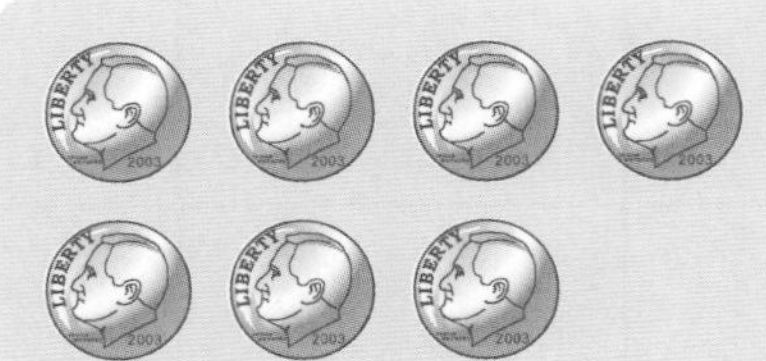

70 cents

80 cents

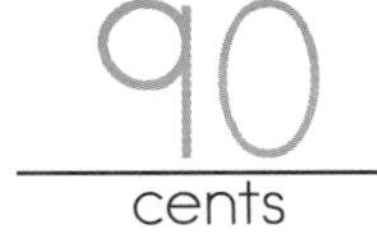

90 cents

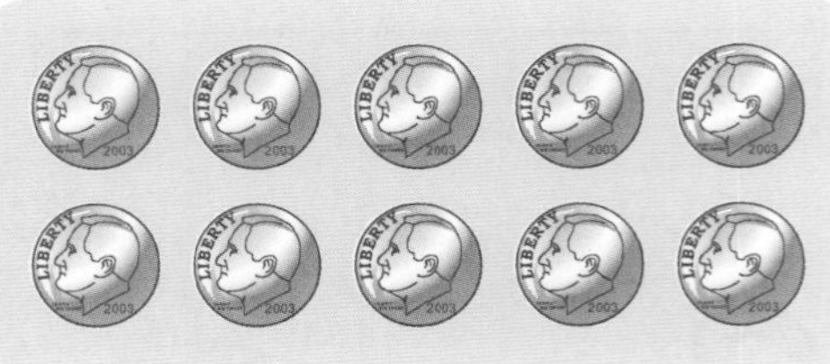

100 cents

10 20 30 40 50 60 70 80 90 100

Help Annie get to the plate of sweets. Count by 10. Color the boxes in order.

10	20	30	40	85
65	50	5	50	65
10	80	70	60	10
25	90	30	15	0
55	100			

Counting by 10

10 20 30 40 50 60 70 80 90 100

Connect the dots.
Start with **10**.

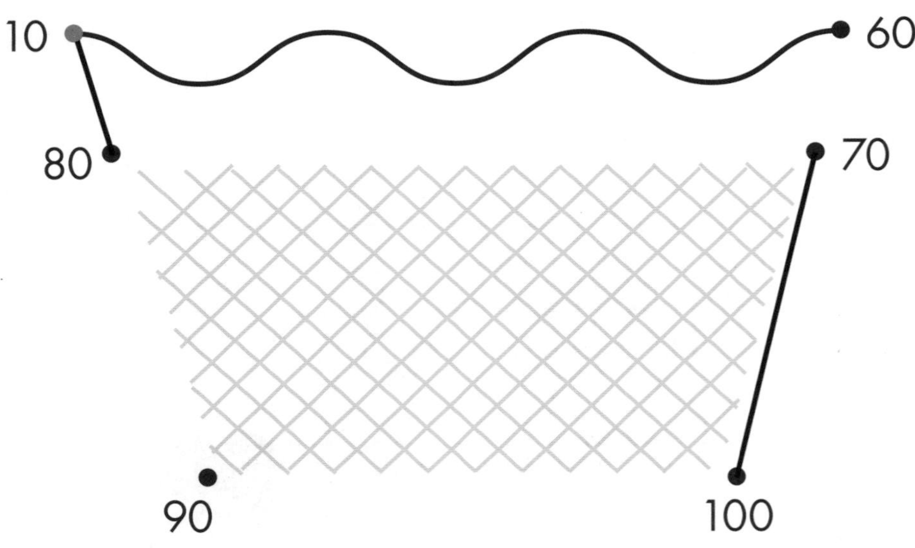

Write the letter for each number to see what the baker is making.

0 = a	10 = b	20 = c	30 = d
40 = e	50 = h	60 = i	70 = k
80 = r	90 = t	100 = y	

10	60	80	90	50	30	0	100
b							

20	0	70	40

Put an **X** on what the baker made.

Trace the Shapes

Trace and color the shapes.

square

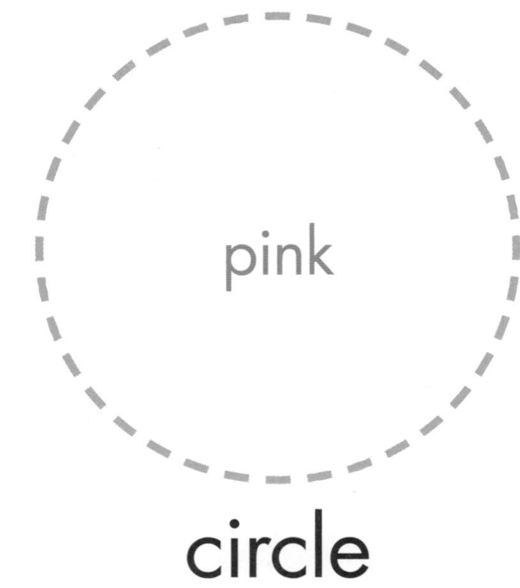

circle

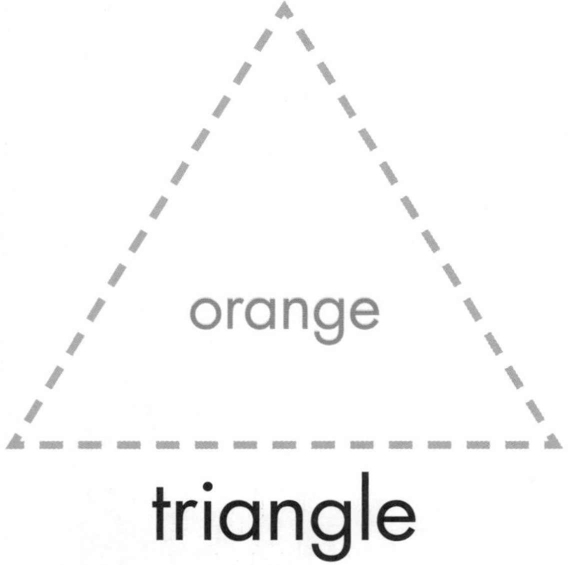

triangle

rectangle

Trace the Shapes

Trace and color the shapes.

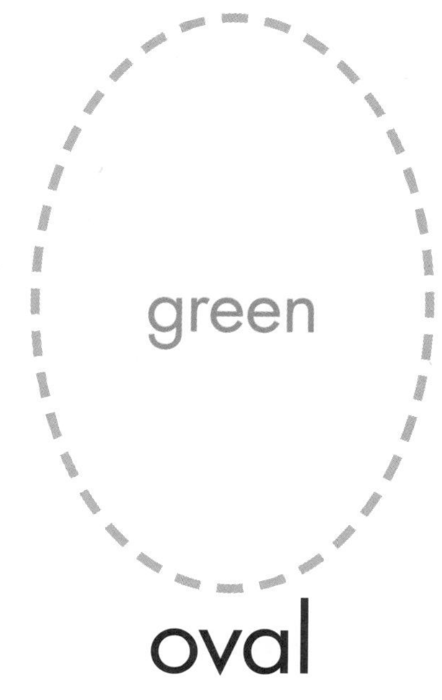

oval

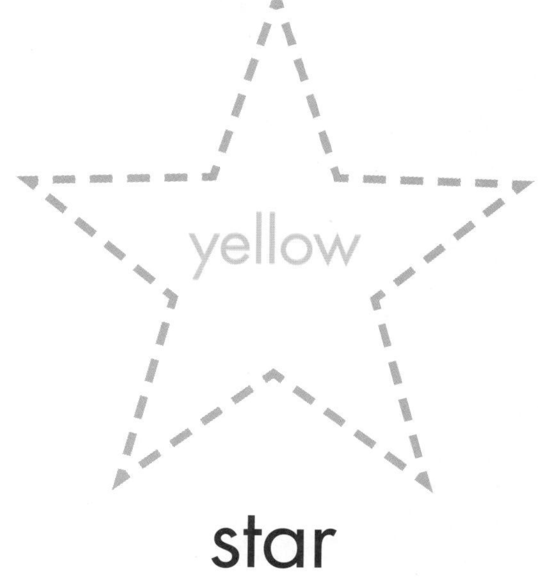

star

heart

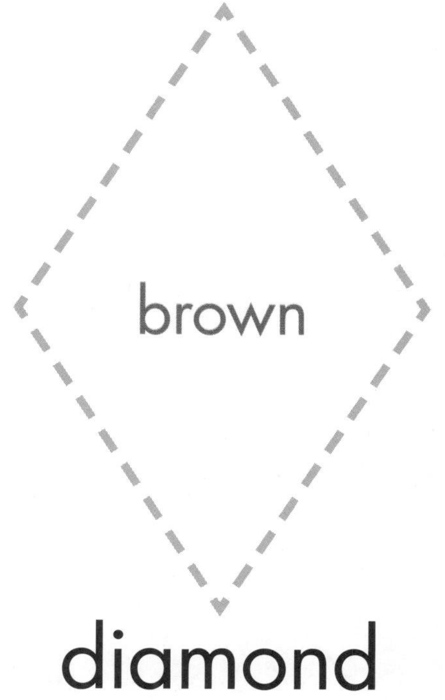

diamond

Find the Shape

Connect the dots.
Start with **1**.

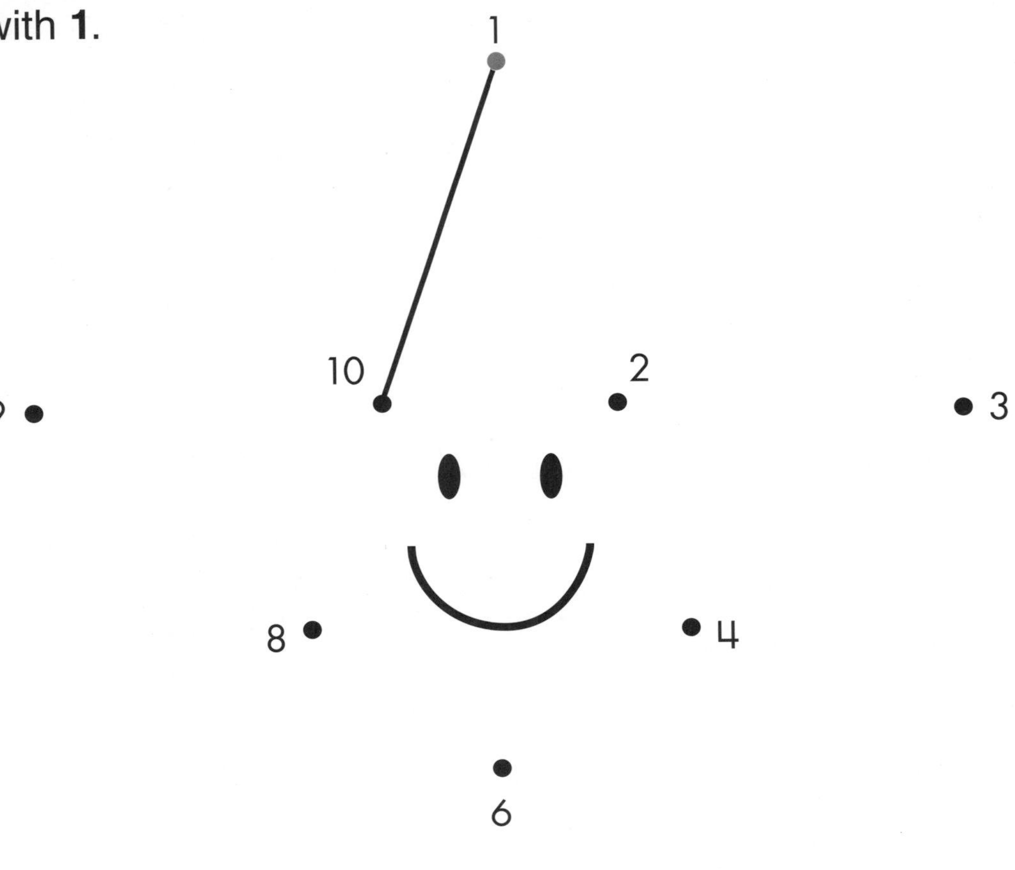

Circle the shape you made.

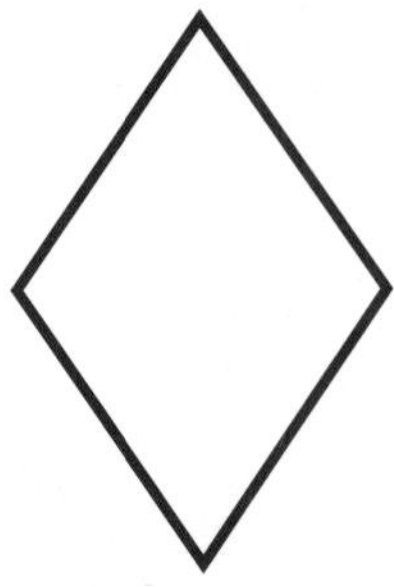

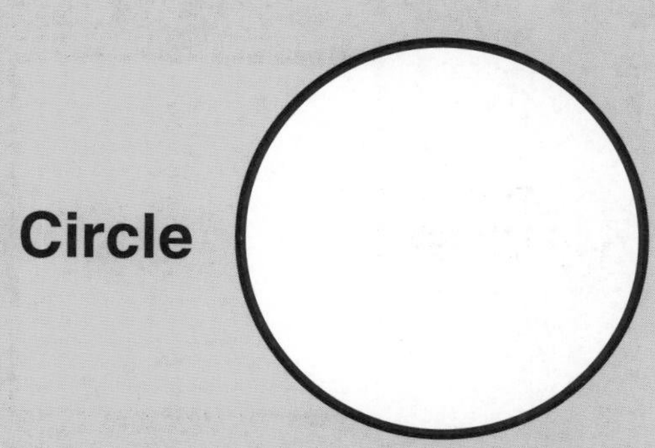

Trace the circles.

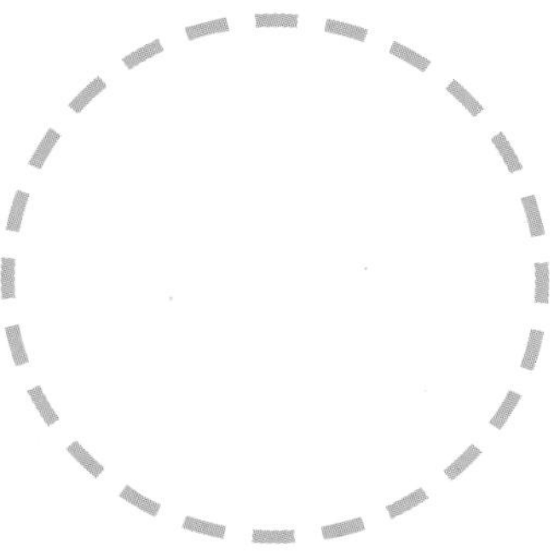
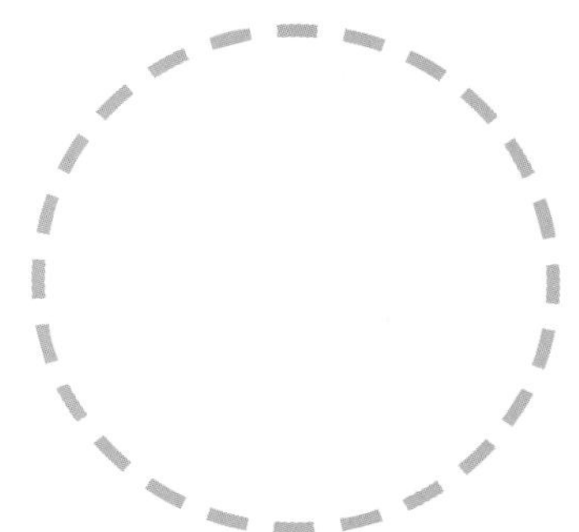
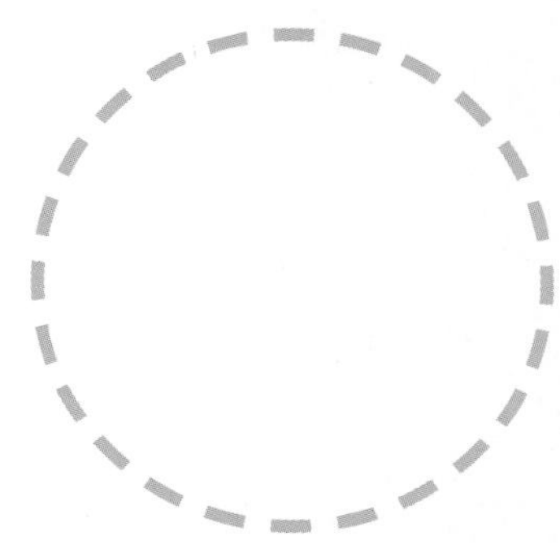

Color the circles.

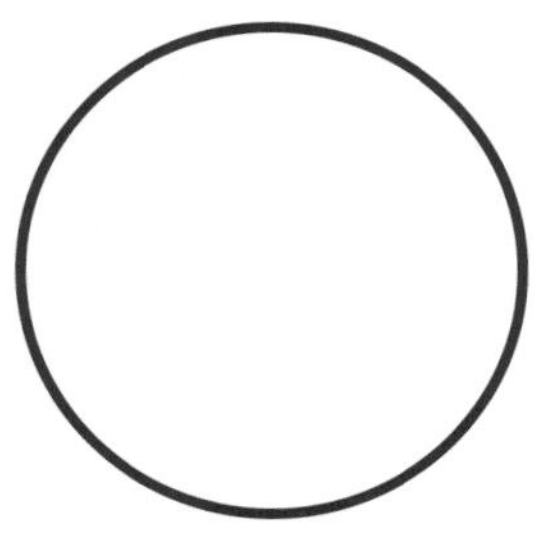

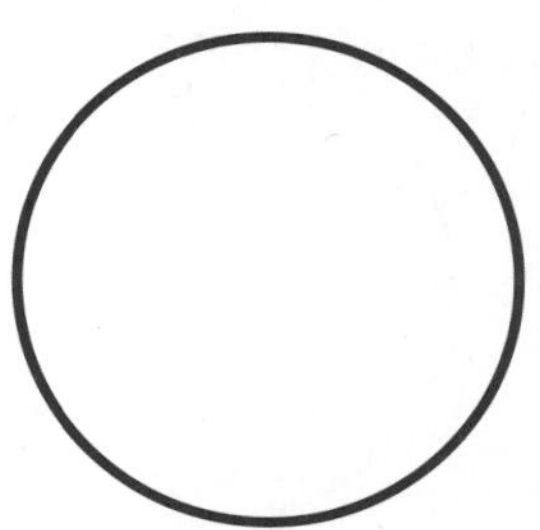
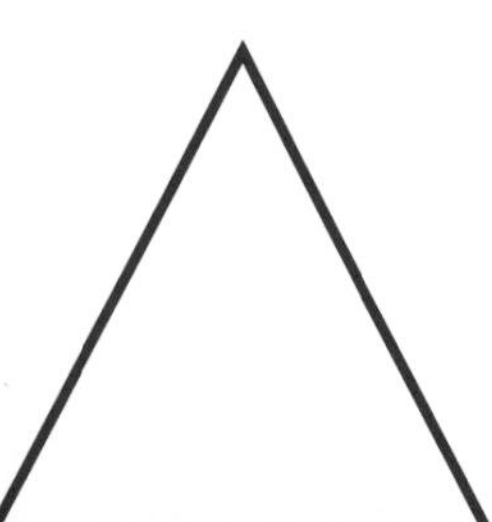
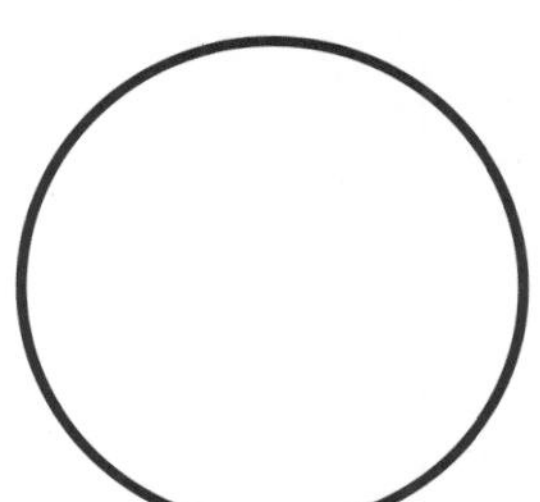

Square 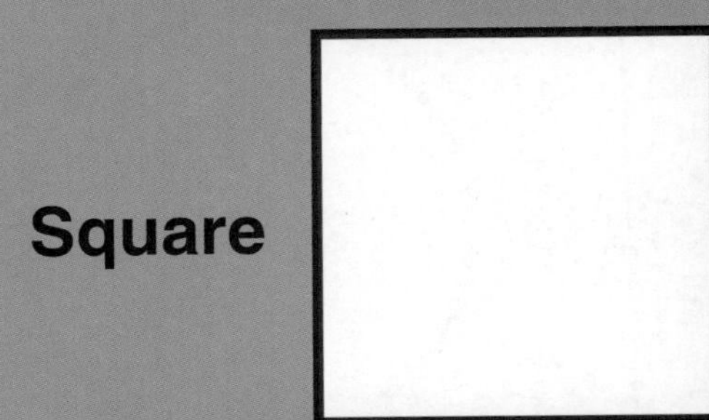

Trace the squares.

Color the squares.

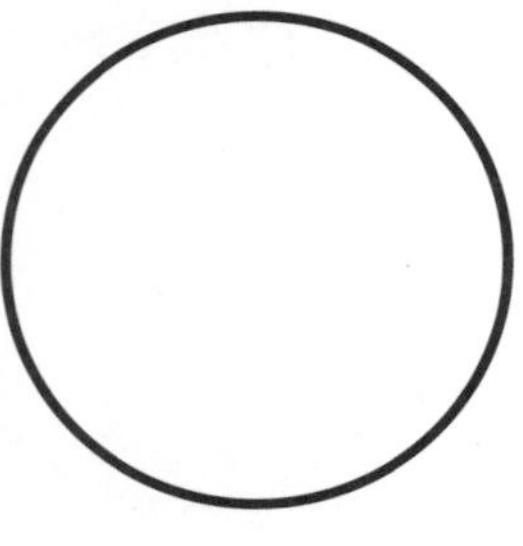  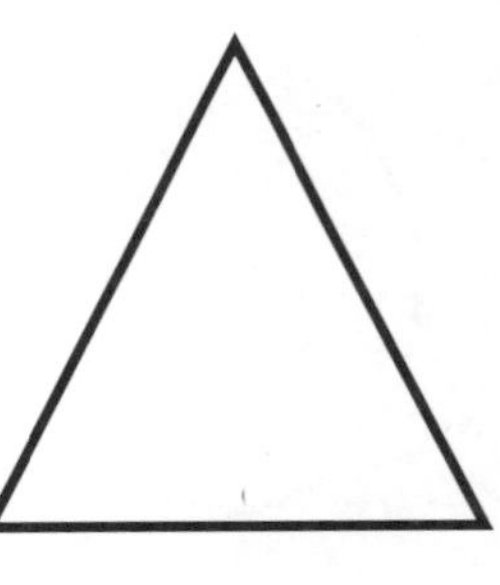

Triangle

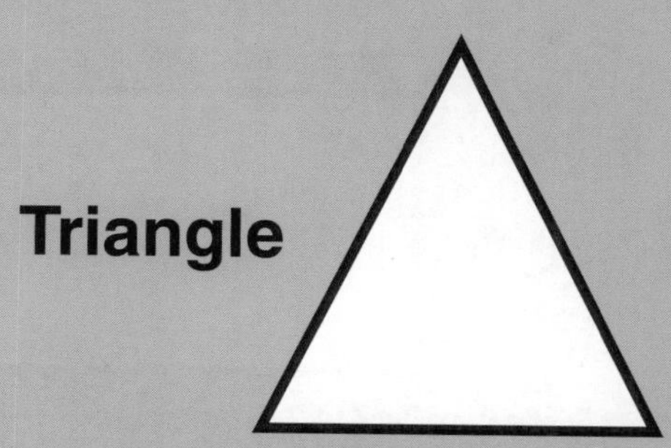

Trace the triangles.

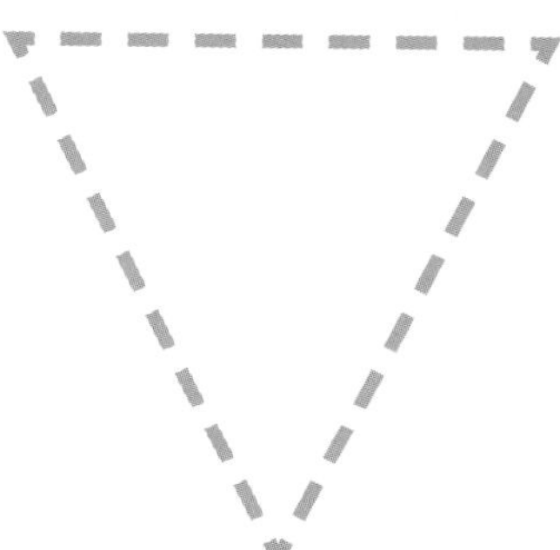

Color the triangles.

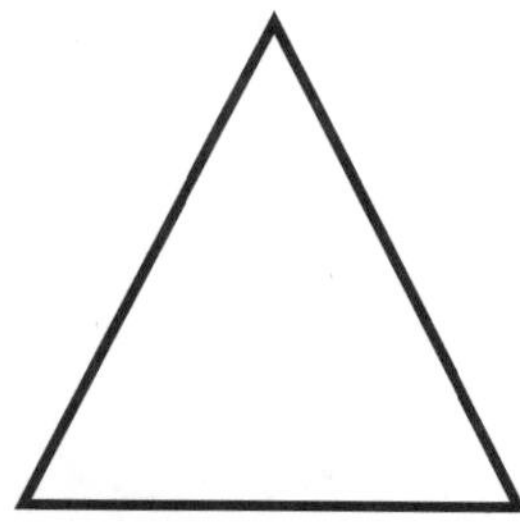
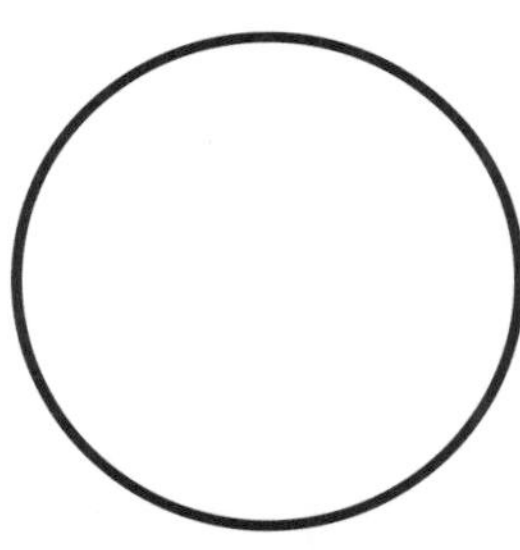

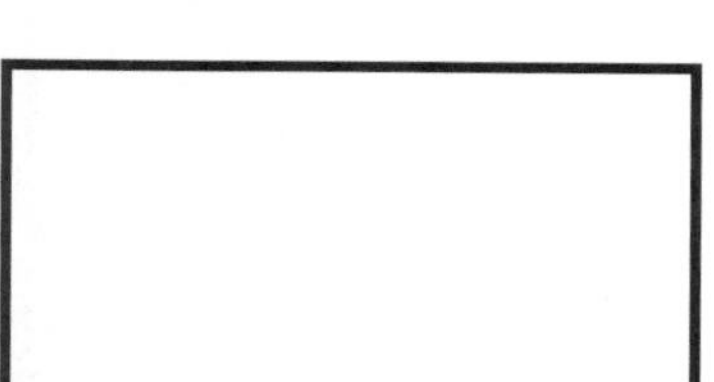

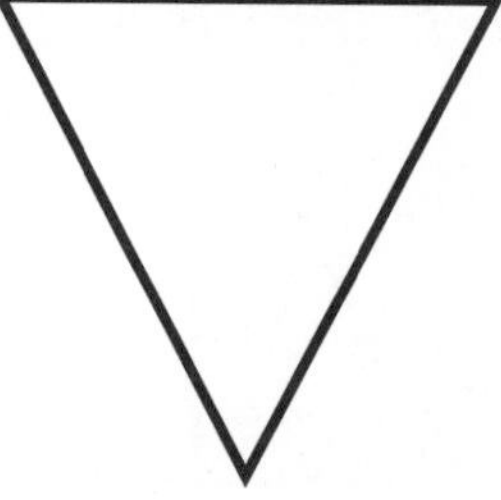

Rectangle

Rectangle

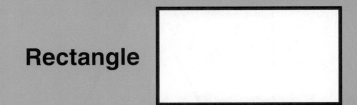

Trace the rectangles.

Color the rectangles.

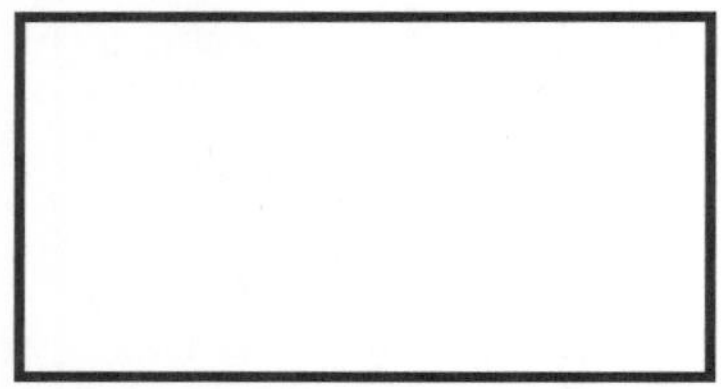

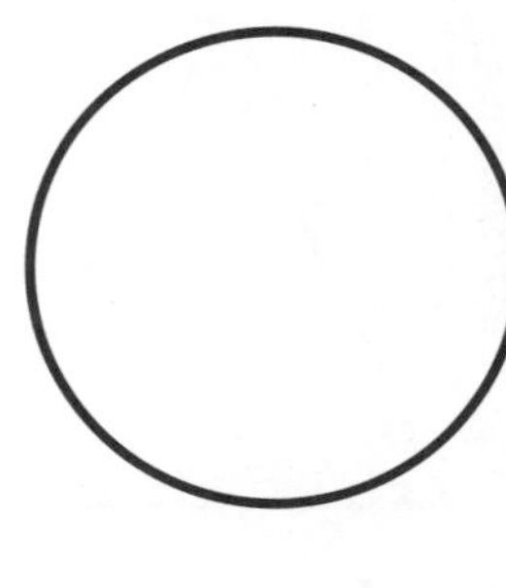
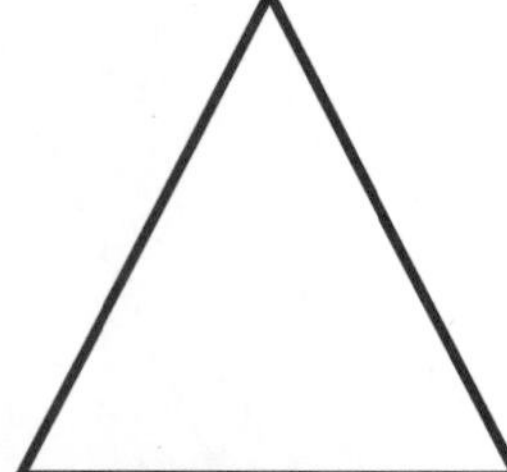
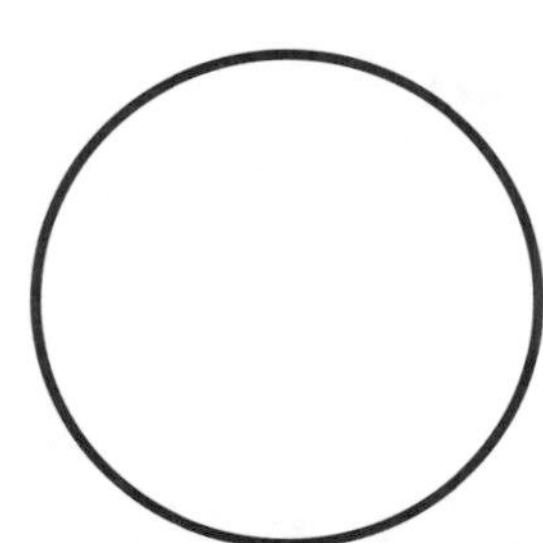
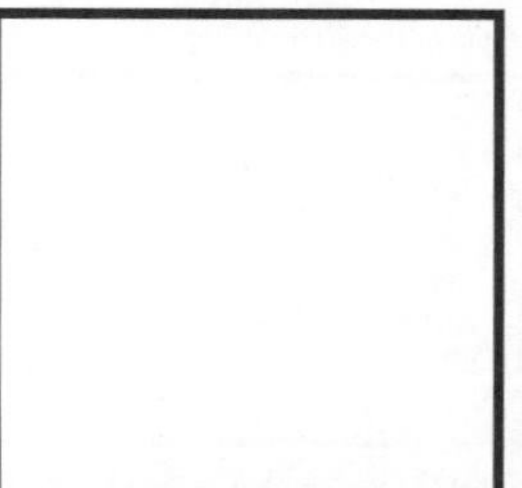

Find the Shapes

Trace the shapes.
Color the circles red.
Color the squares blue.

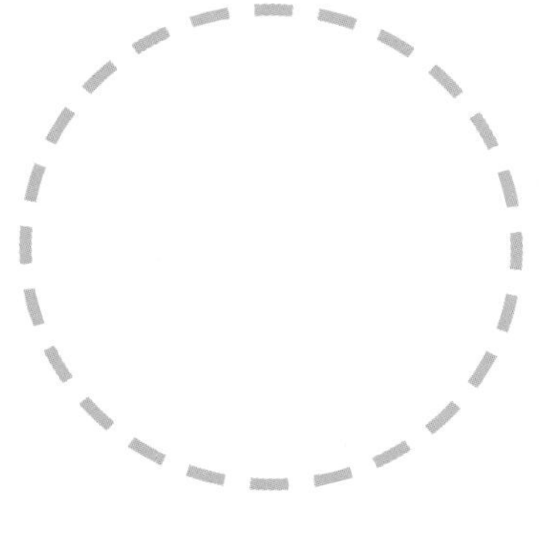

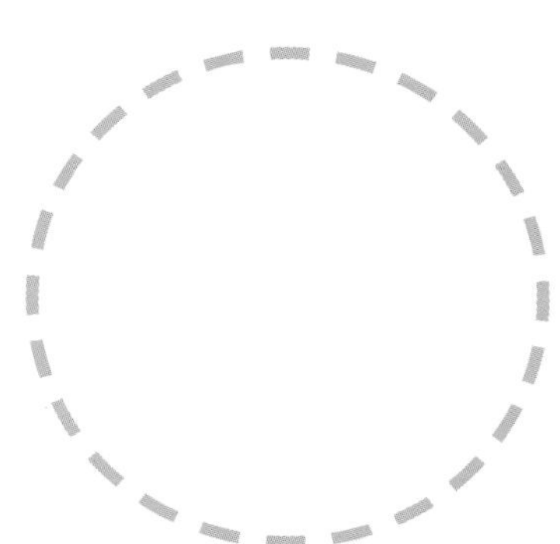

Trace the name.

Find the Shapes

▶ Trace the shapes.
Color the rectangles yellow.
Color the triangles purple.

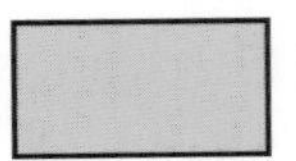
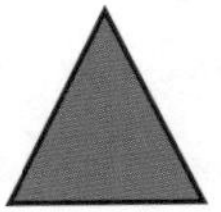

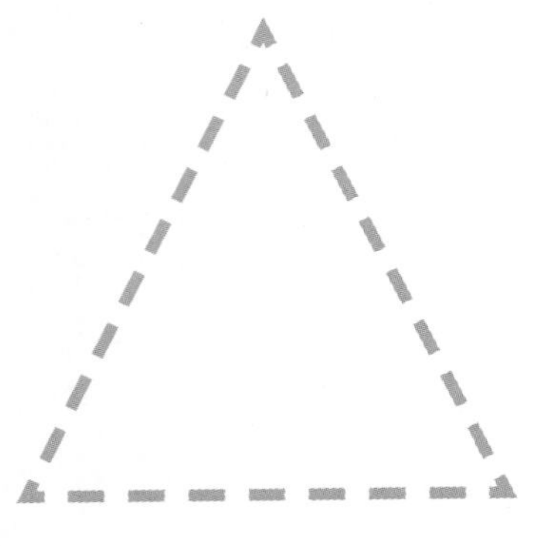
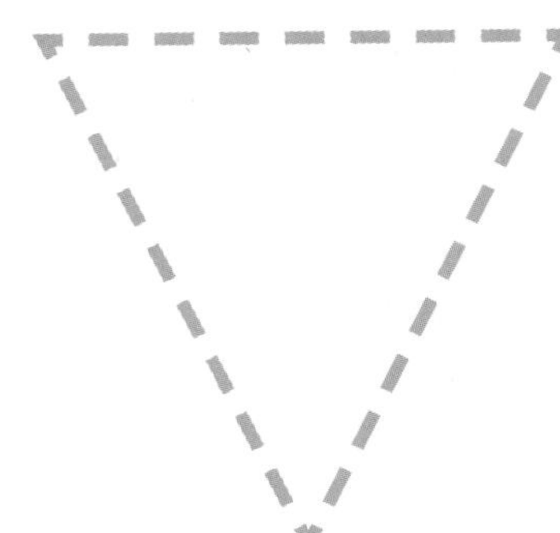

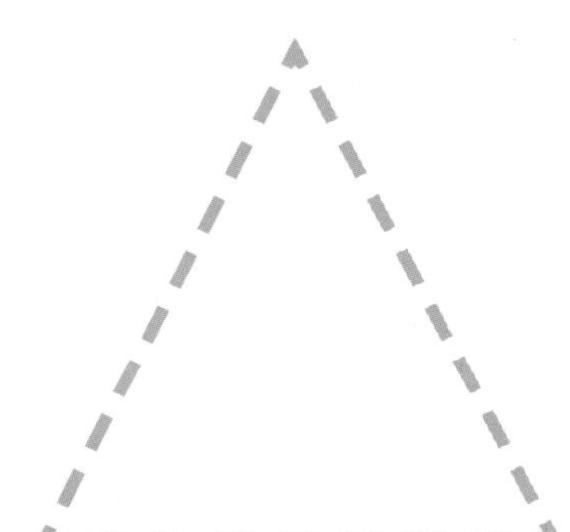

▶ Trace the name.

Make a Match

Draw a line to make a match.

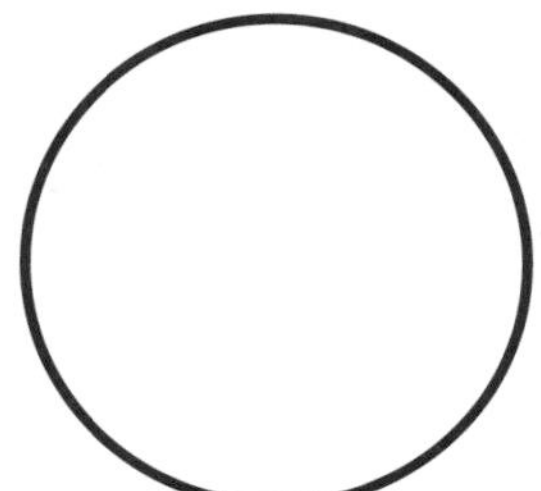

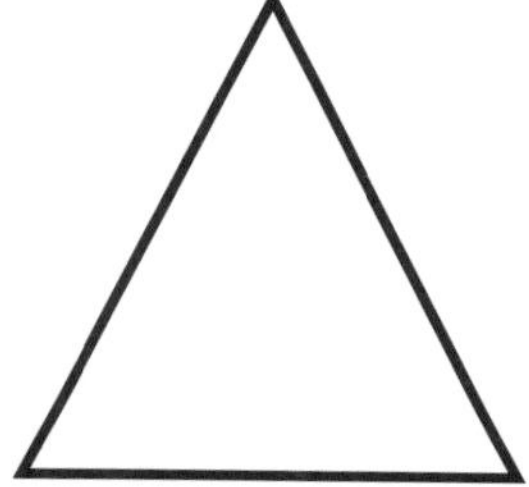

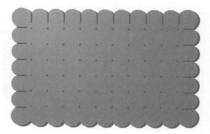

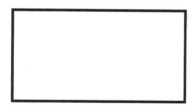

Find the Shapes

Color the squares red.
Color the circles yellow.
Color the rectangles blue.

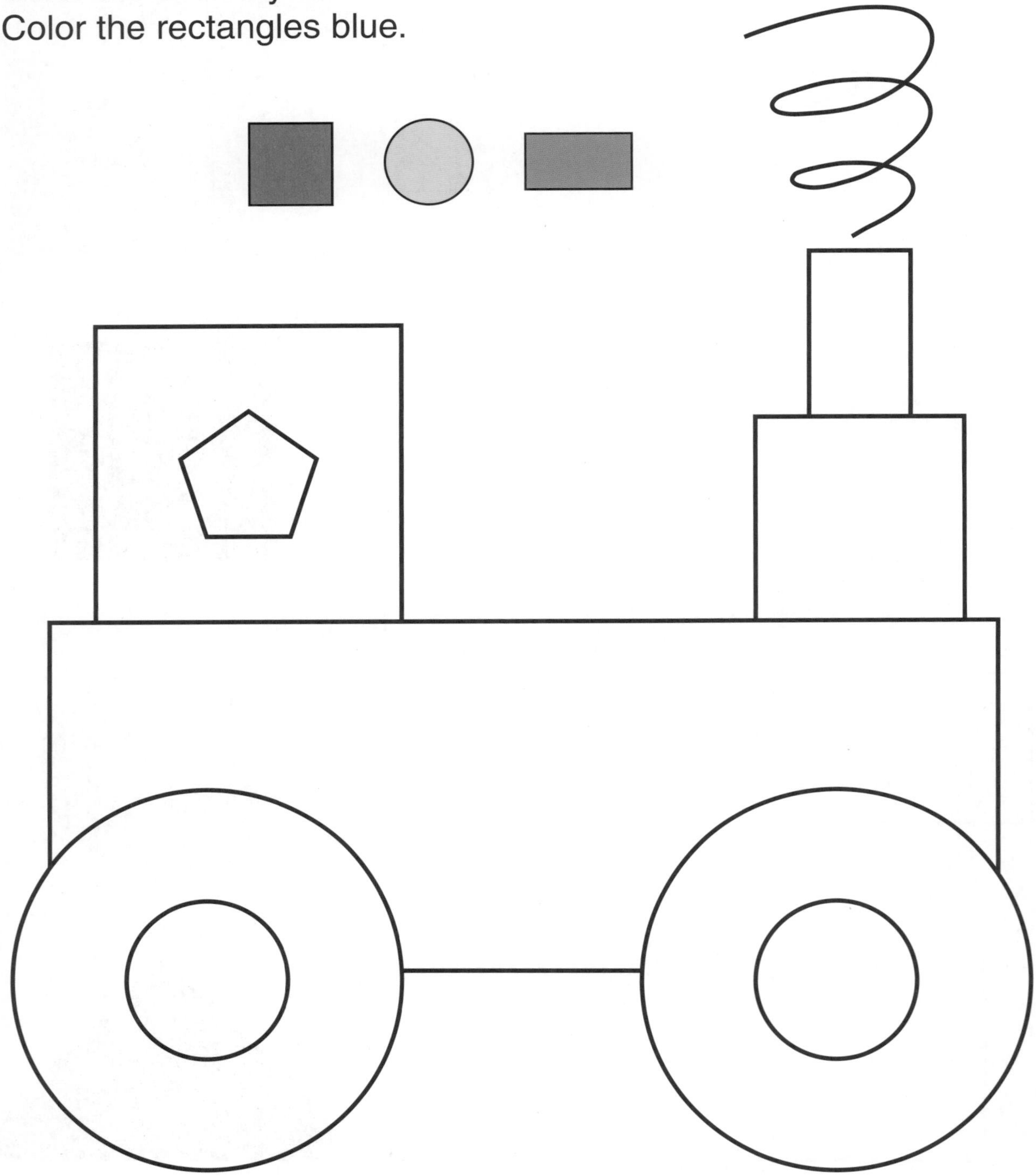

Find the Shapes

Color the circles brown.
Color the squares green.
Color the rectangles blue.
Color the triangles black.

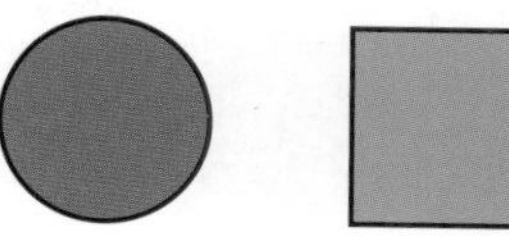

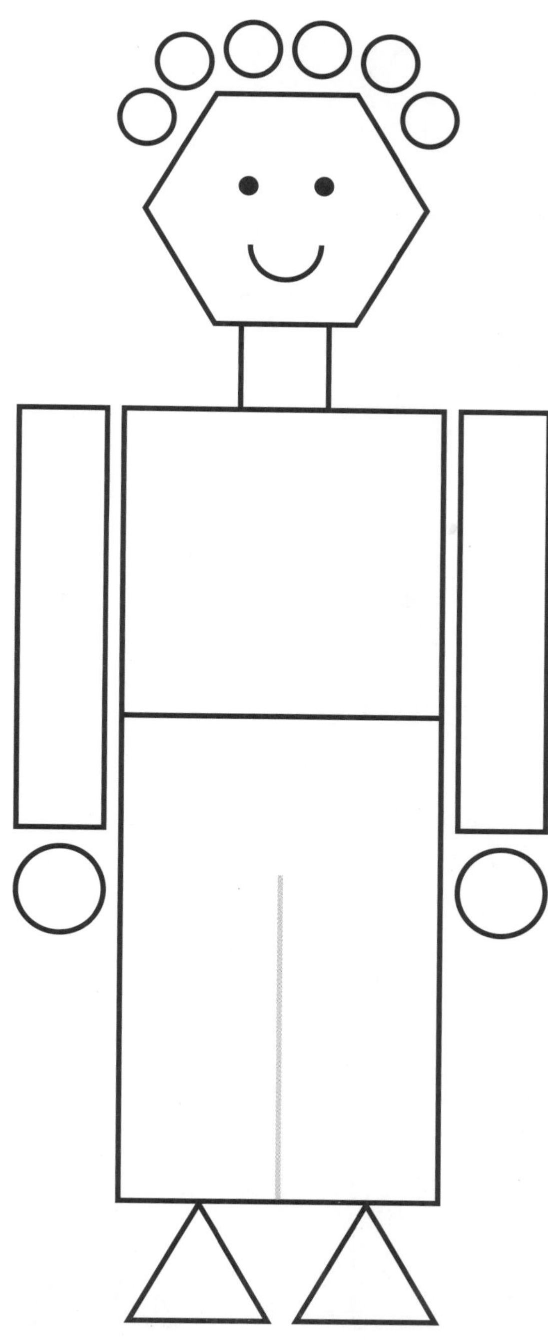

Find the Shapes

▶ Connect the dots.
Start with **1**.

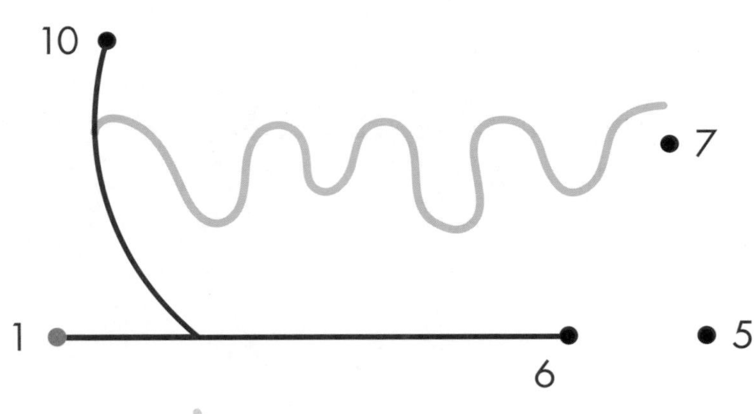

▶ Circle the shapes you made.

Find the Shapes

Color the circles yellow.
Color the ovals blue.
Color the hearts pink.

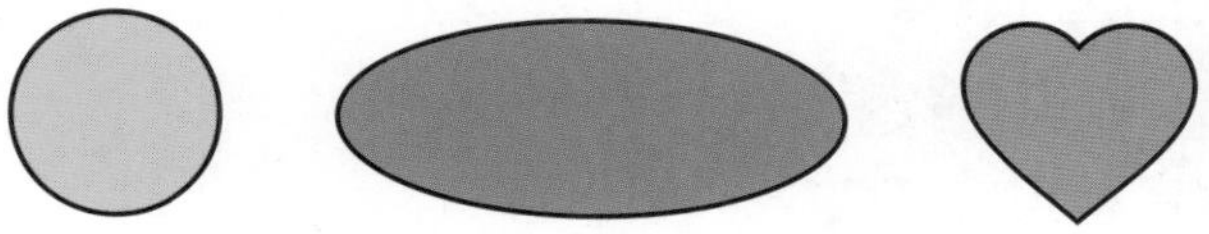

Find the Shapes

Connect the dots and color.
Start with **1**.
Color the circles yellow.
Color the triangles red.
Color the rectangles blue.

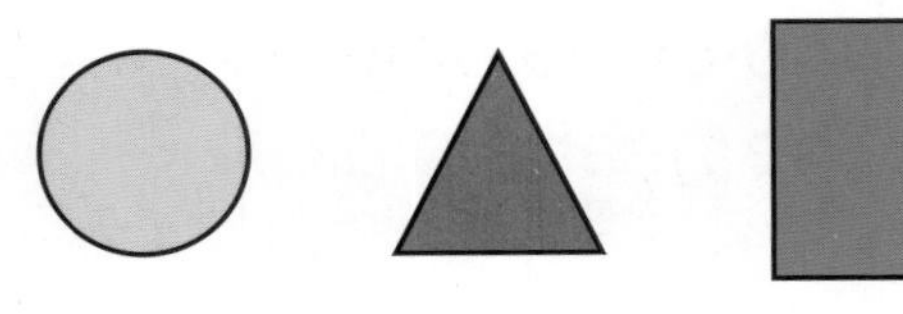

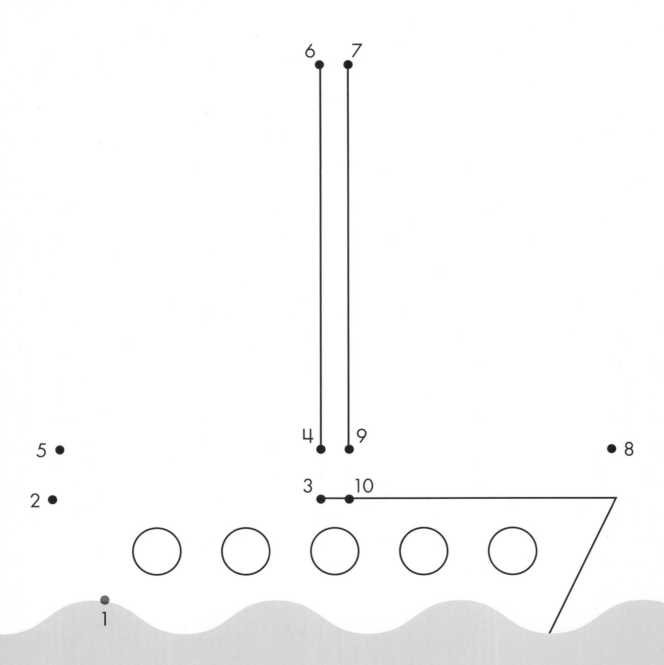

Make a Graph

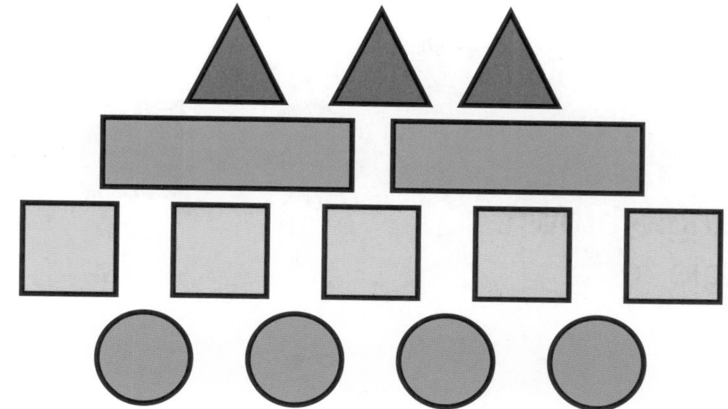

Color one space for each shape.

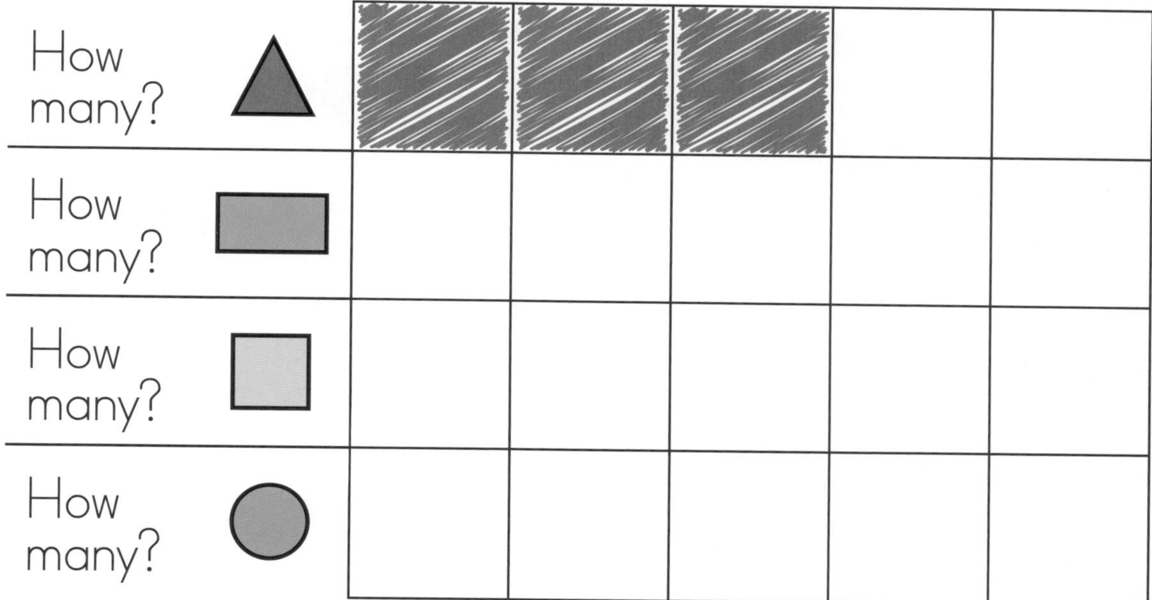

Circle the shape that has the most.

Circle the shape that has the least.

Find the Shapes

Connect the dots.
Start with **1**.
Color the circle black.
Color the square green.
Color the rectangle brown.
Color the triangle red.

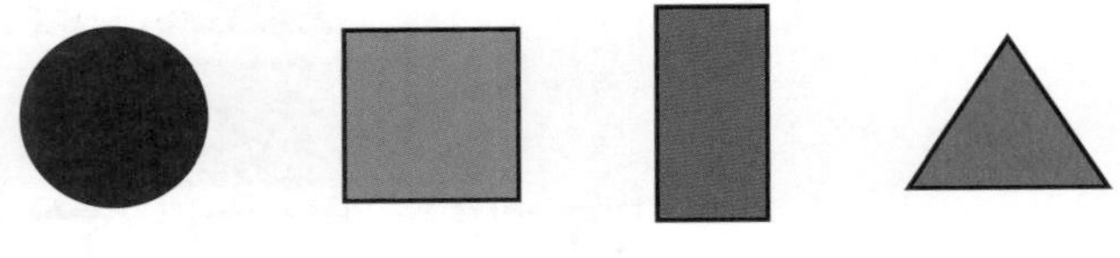

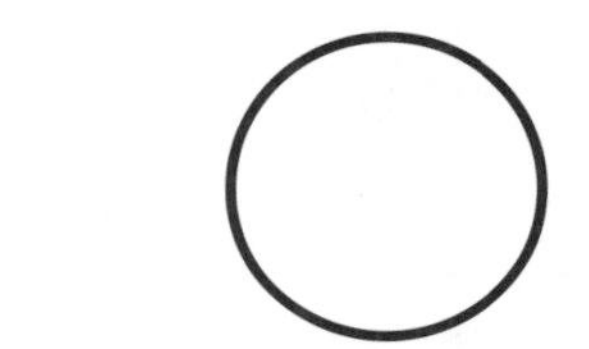

8 7 4 3

6 5

A Shape Picture

Add shapes to make a picture.

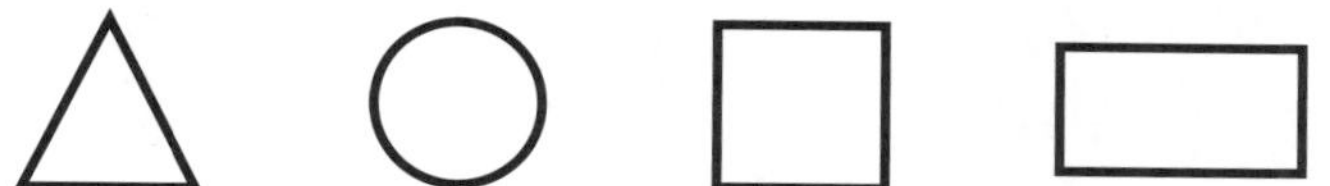

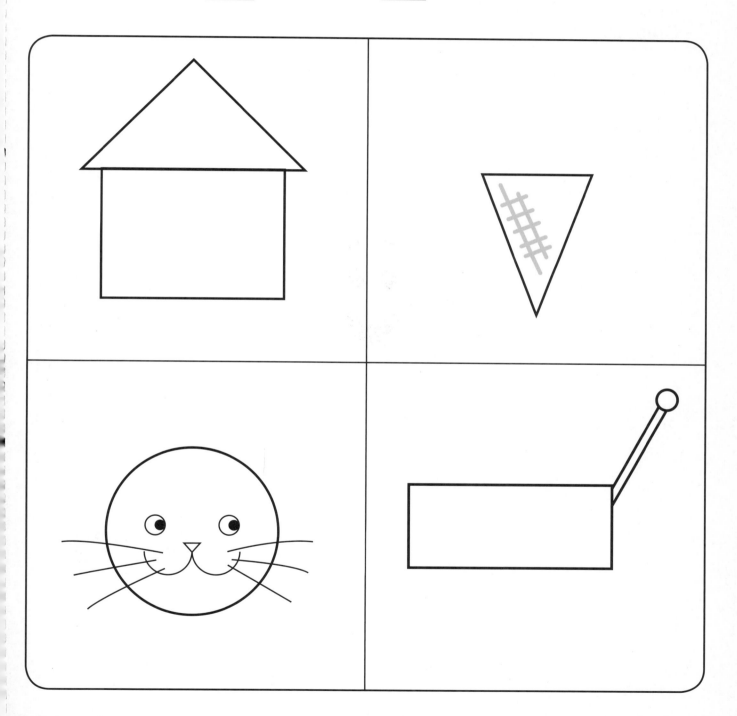

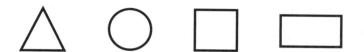

Find the Shapes

Connect the dots.
Start with **1**.
Color the circles yellow.
Color the squares green.
Color the rectangles blue.
Color the triangles red.

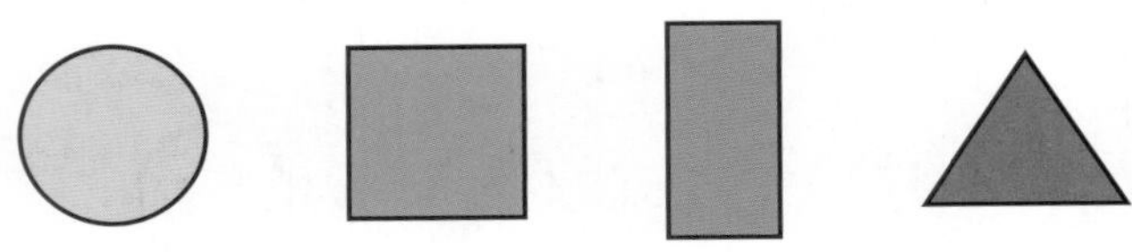

8

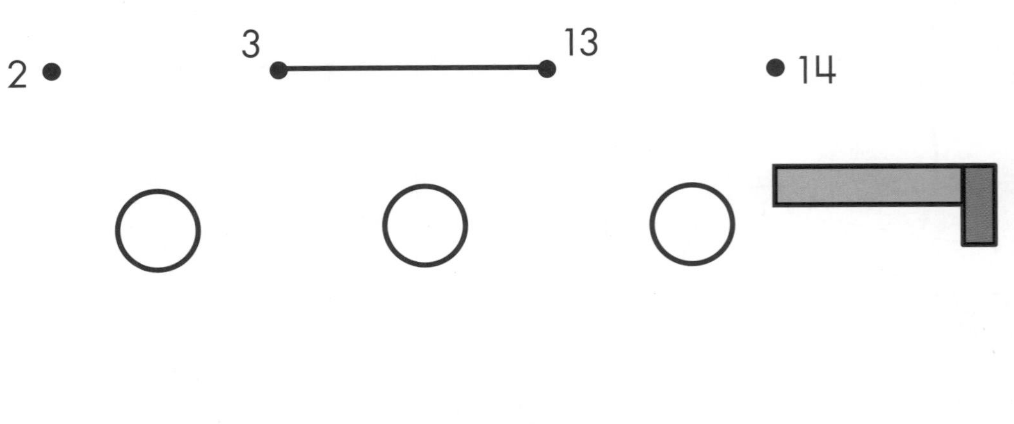

Color the shapes.
Follow the pattern.

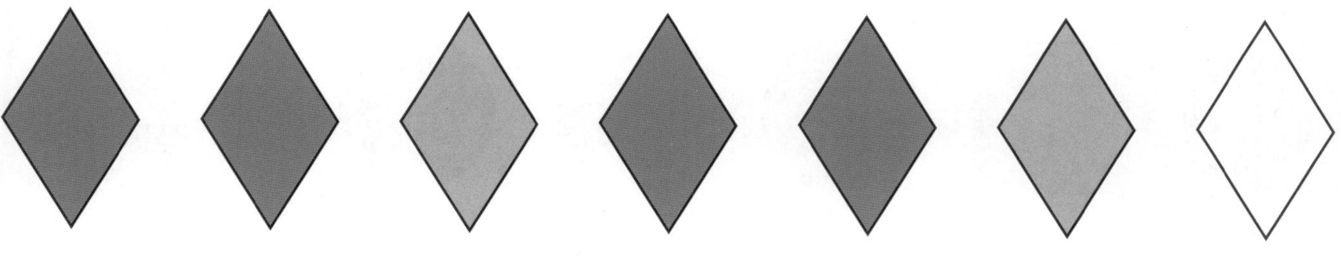

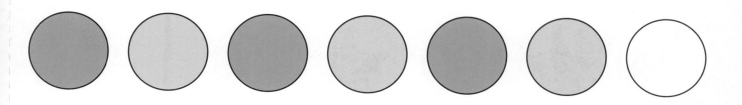

Patterning

Circle the picture that comes next.
Follow the pattern.

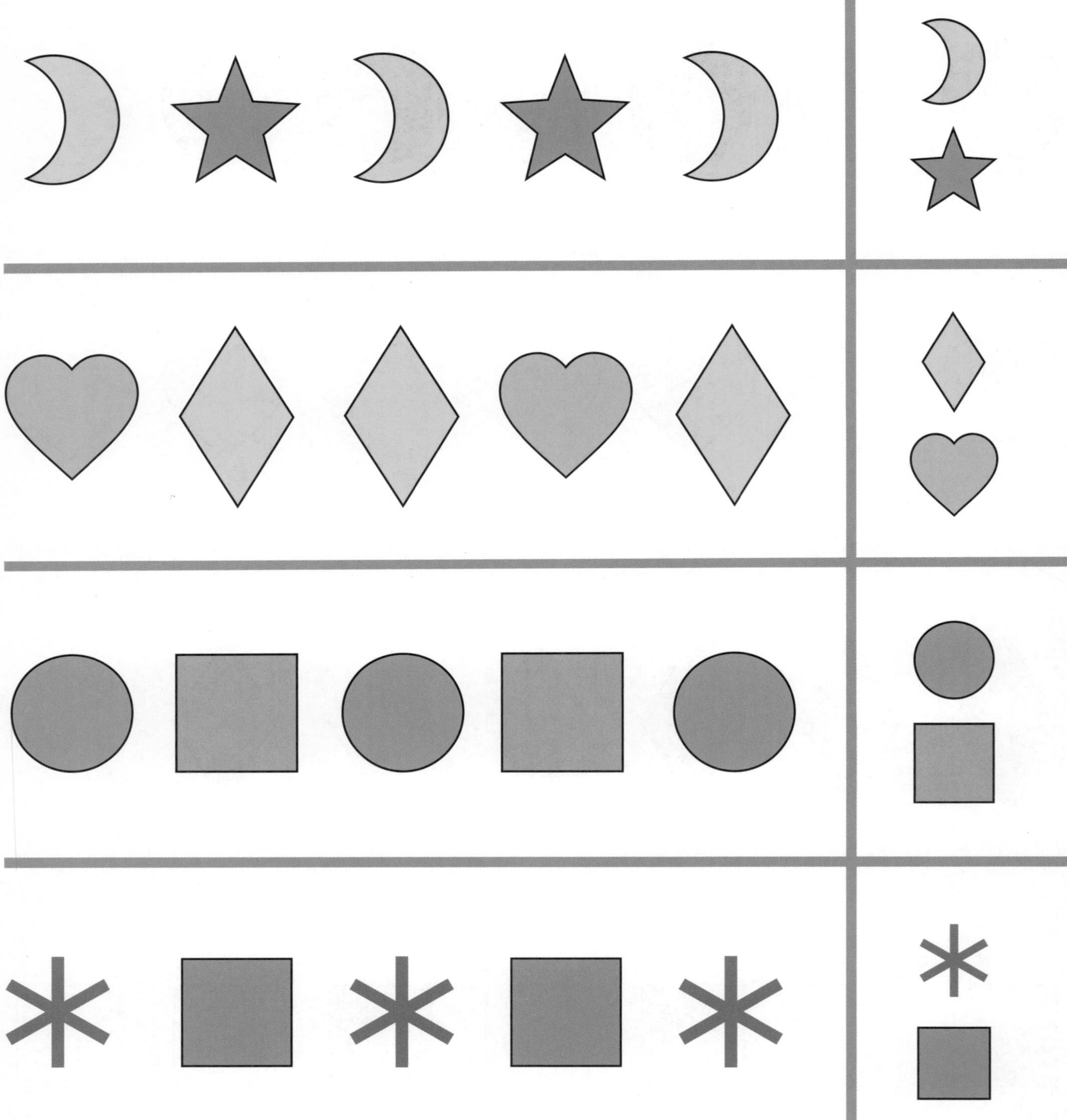

Color the shapes.
Follow the pattern.

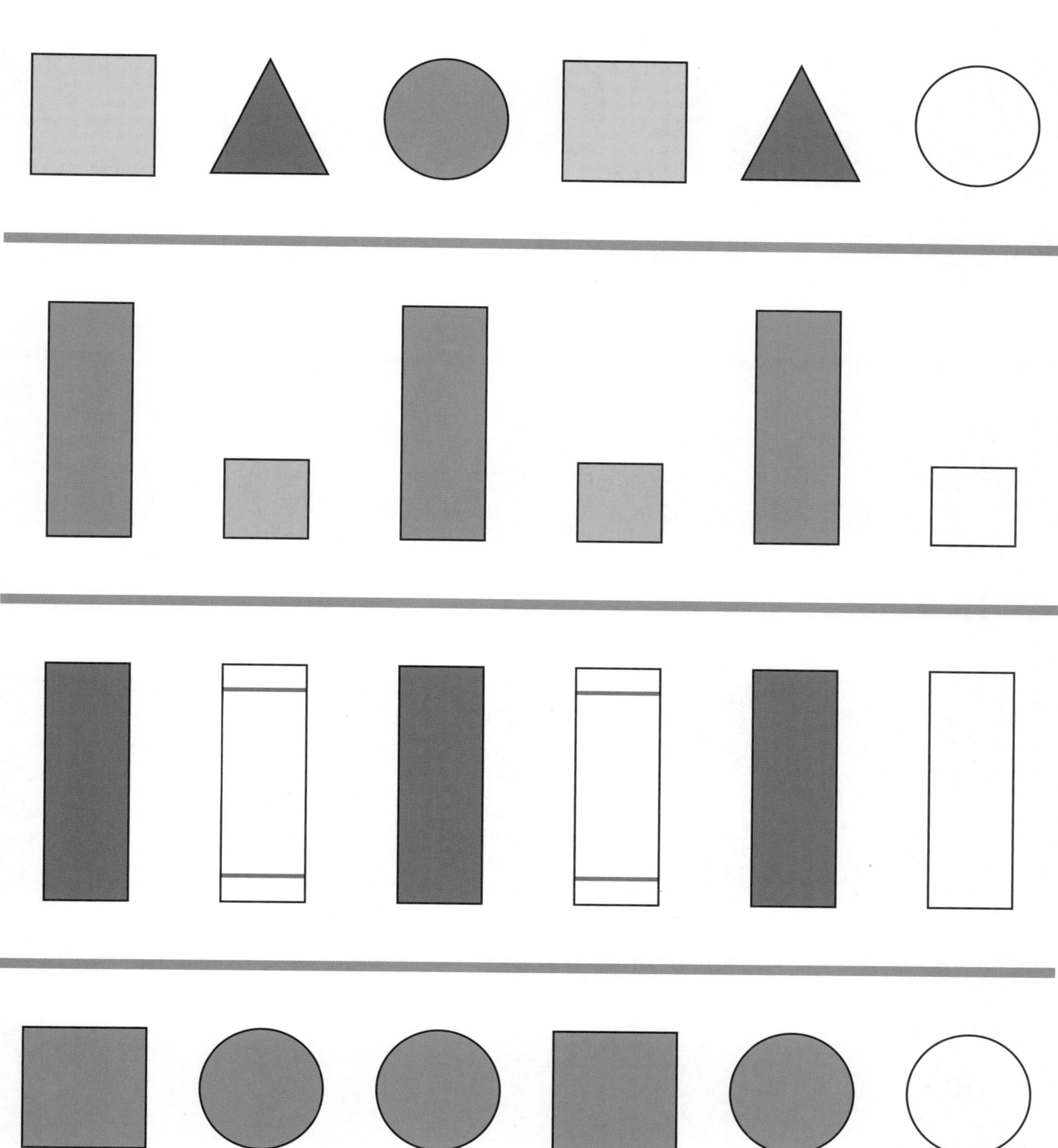

Patterning

Draw the picture that comes next.
Follow the pattern.

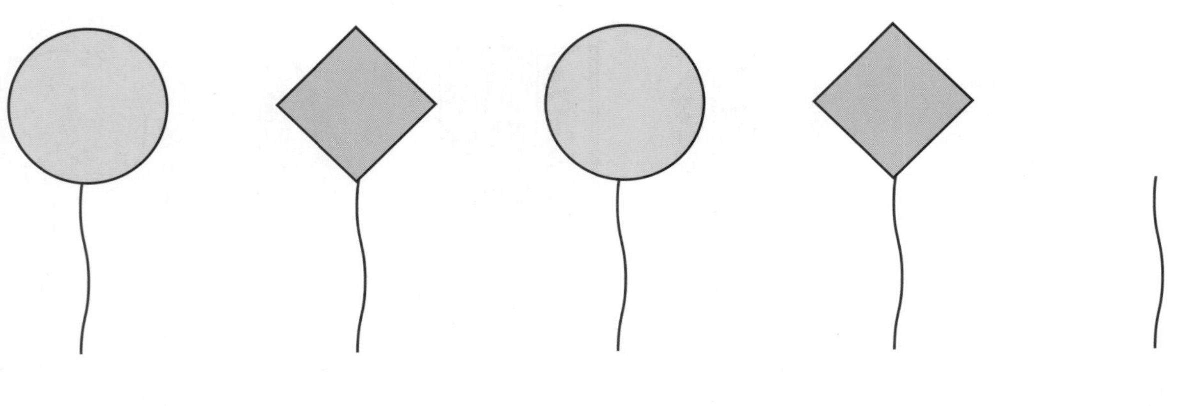

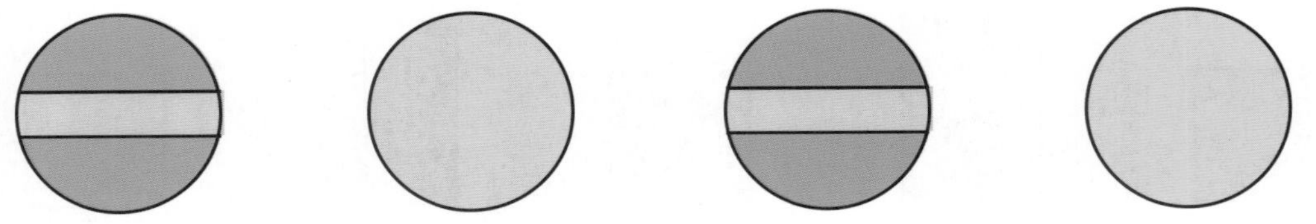

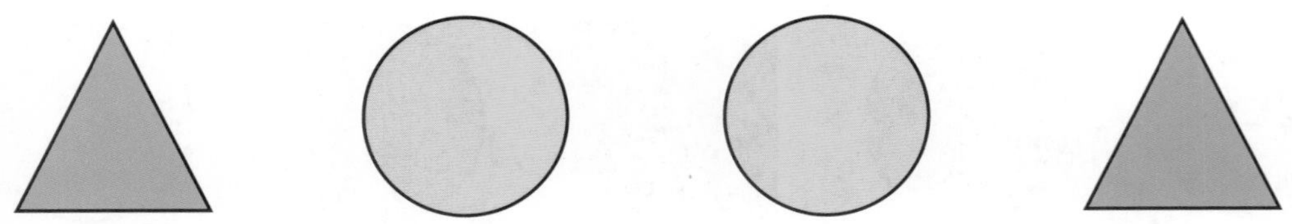

Circle the picture that comes next.
Follow the pattern.

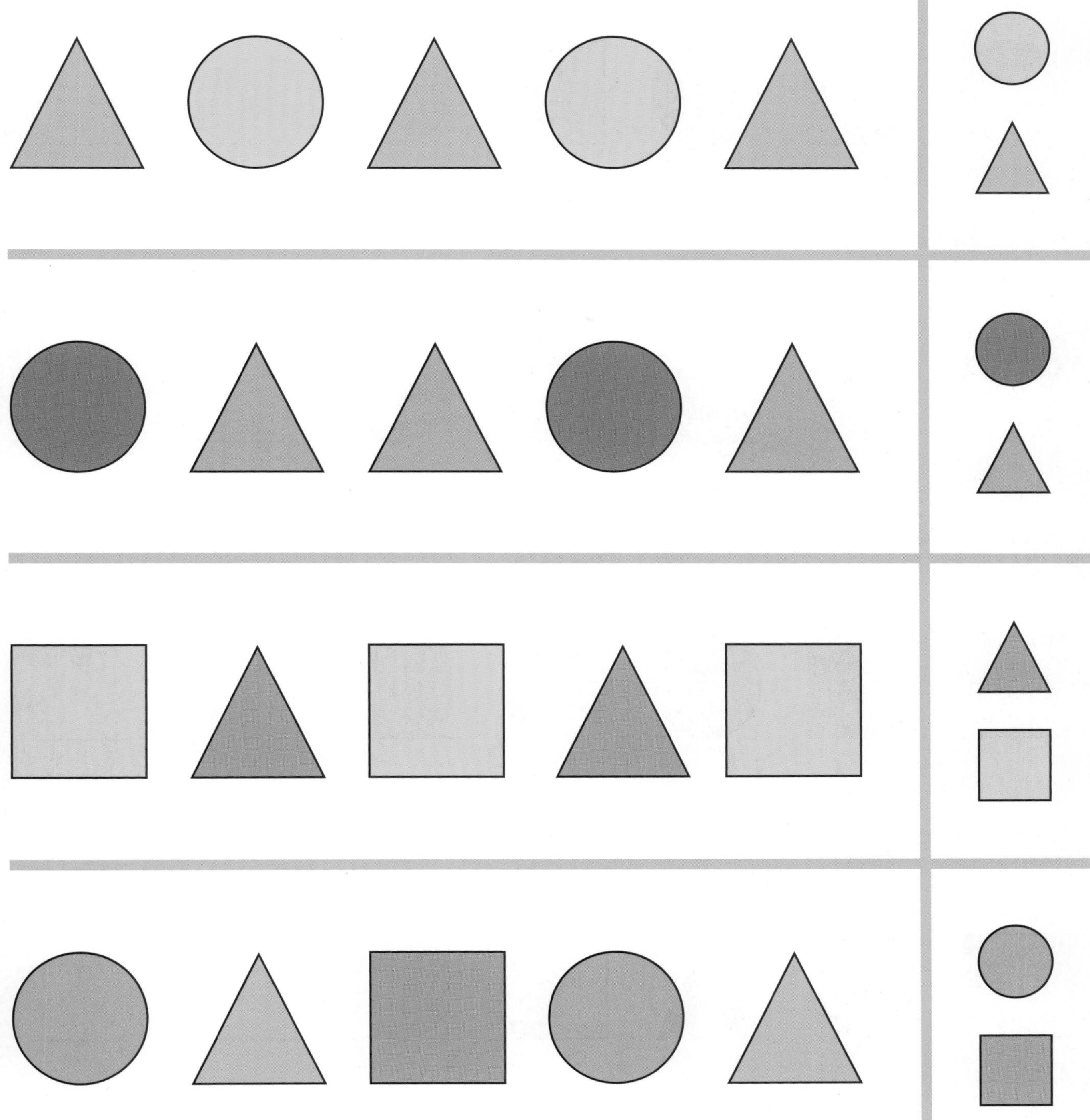

Patterning

Draw the shapes that come next.
Follow the pattern.

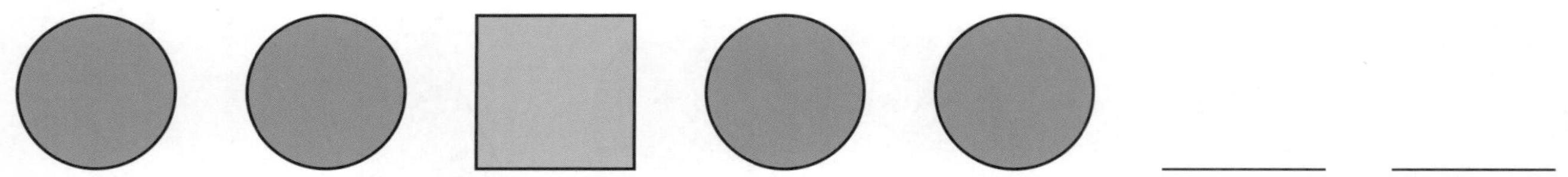

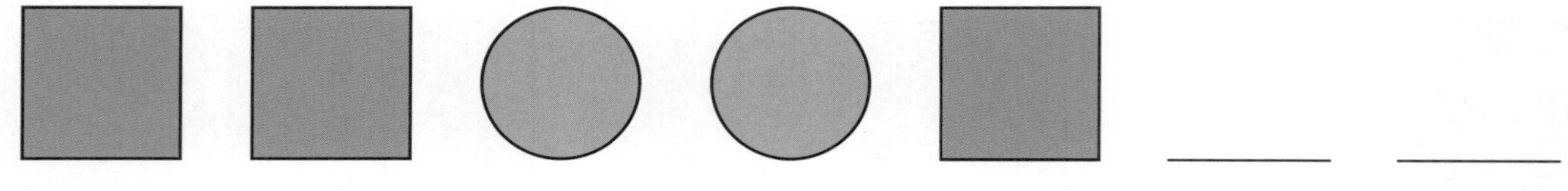

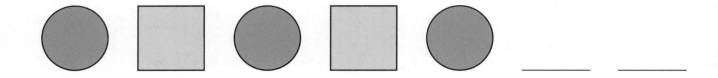

Draw a pattern.
Color it.

Number Patterns

Write the numbers that come next.
Follow the pattern.

1	2	3	4		
10	11	12	13		
12	11	10	9		
6	5	4	3		

Number Patterns

Write the numbers that come next.
Follow the pattern.

1 1 2 1 1 2 ☐ ☐

1 2 3 1 2 3 ☐ ☐

5 5 10 5 5 10 ☐ ☐

10 9 8 7 6 5 ☐ ☐

Money Patterns

Circle the coin that comes next.
Follow the pattern.

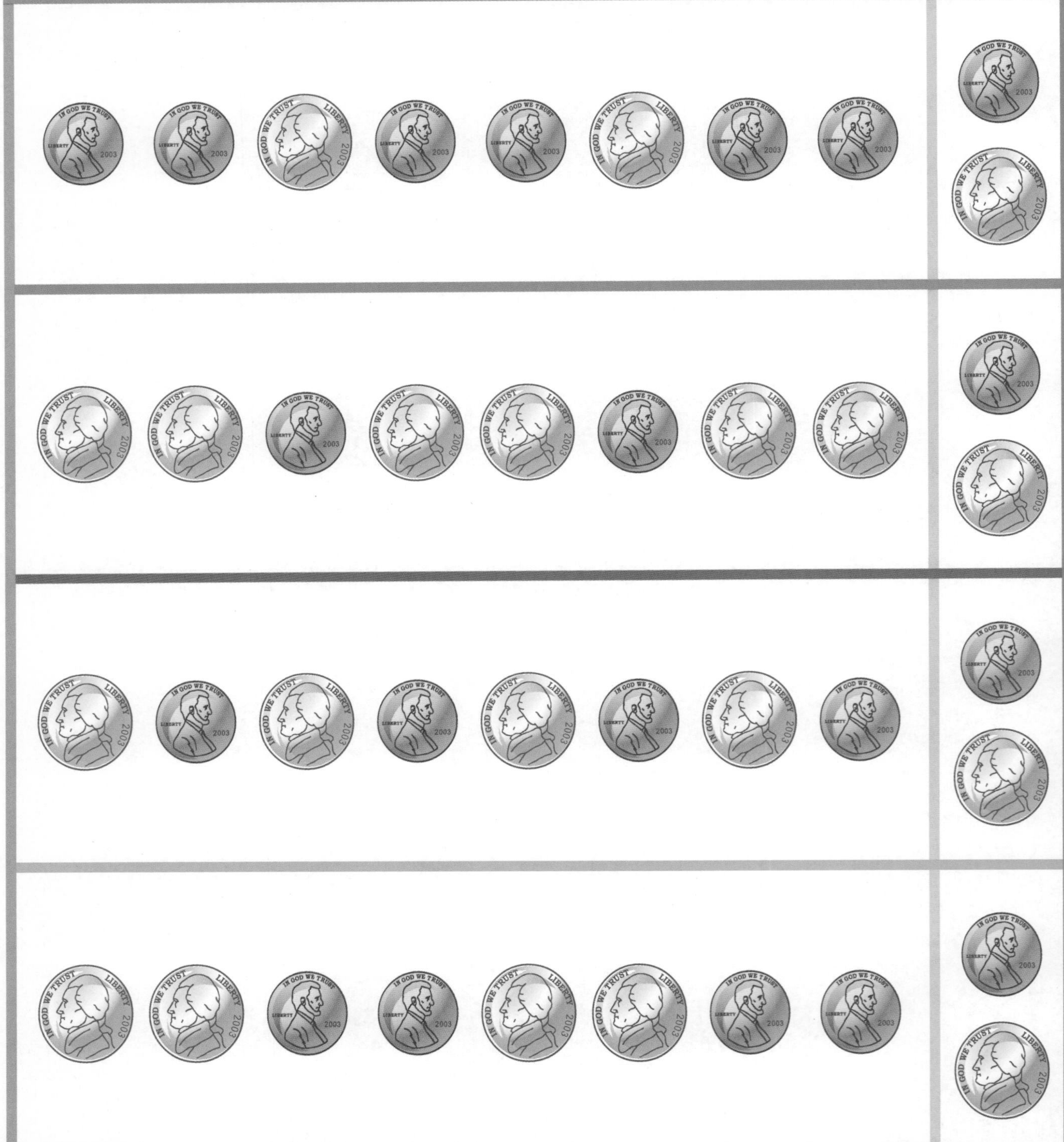

Picture Pattern

▶ Color the boxes that have a △ to find the pattern.

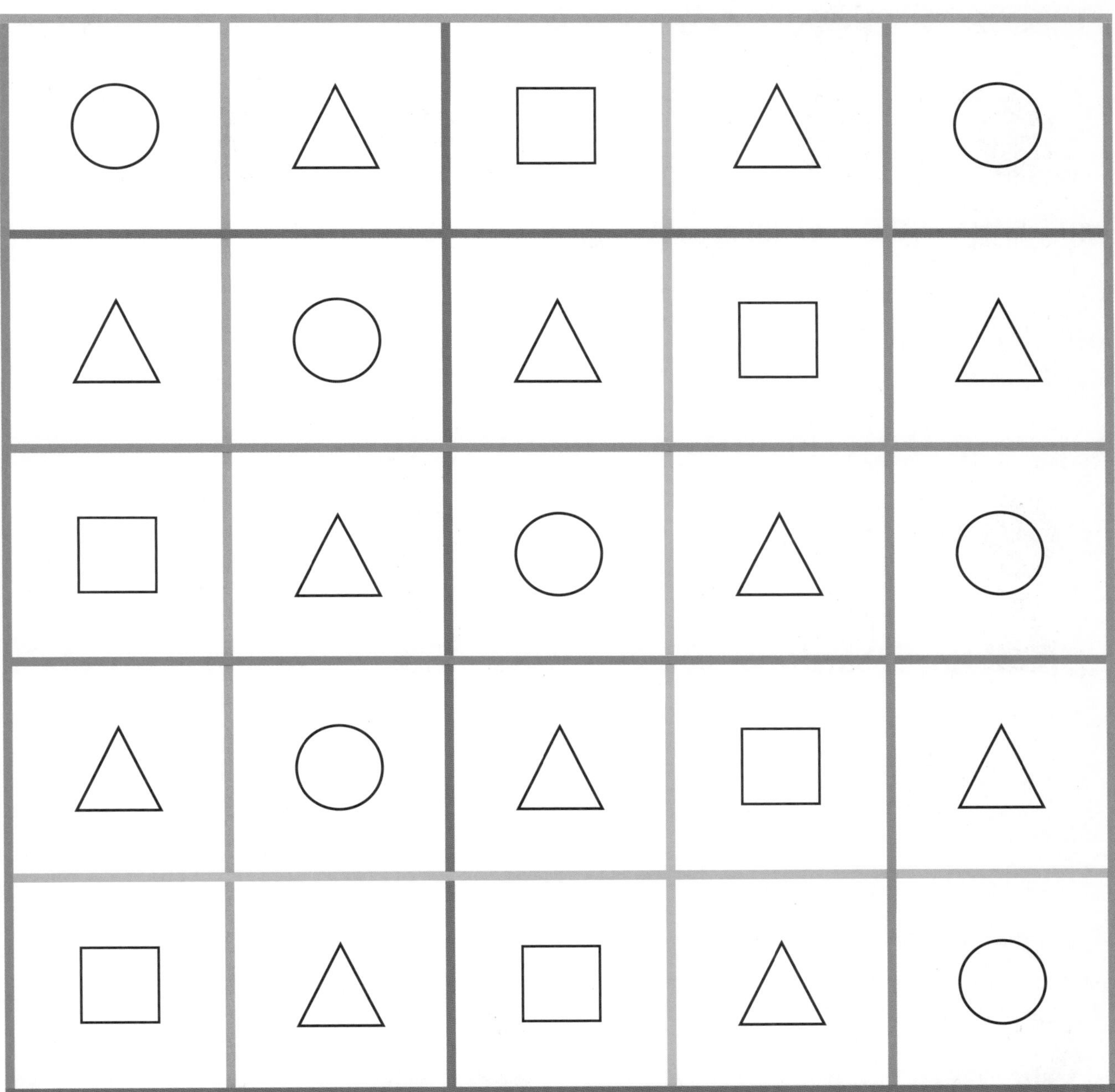

Add

Add the numbers.

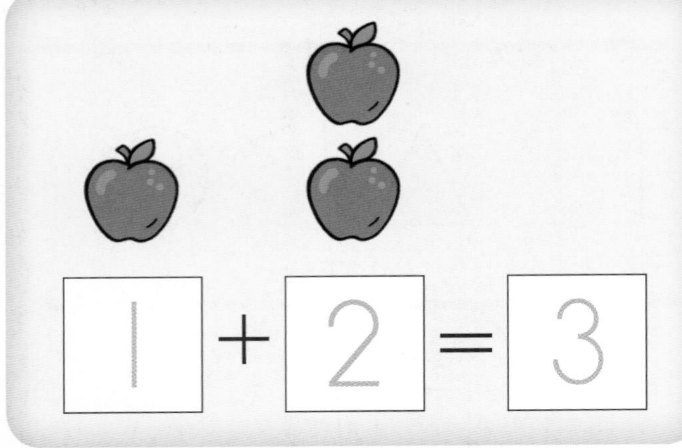

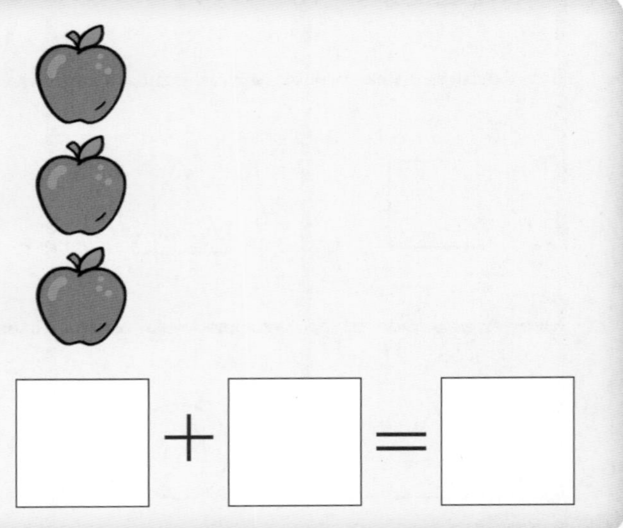

Draw 1 more. Count.

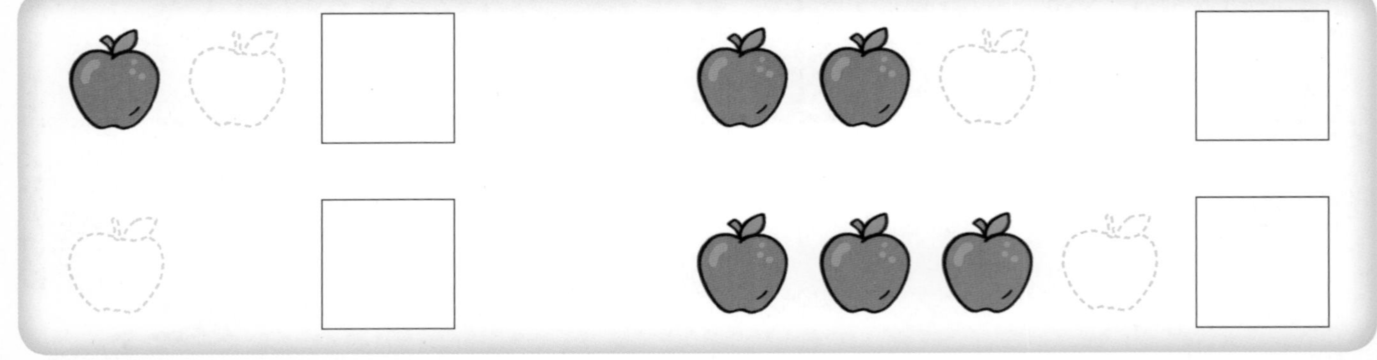

Add the numbers.

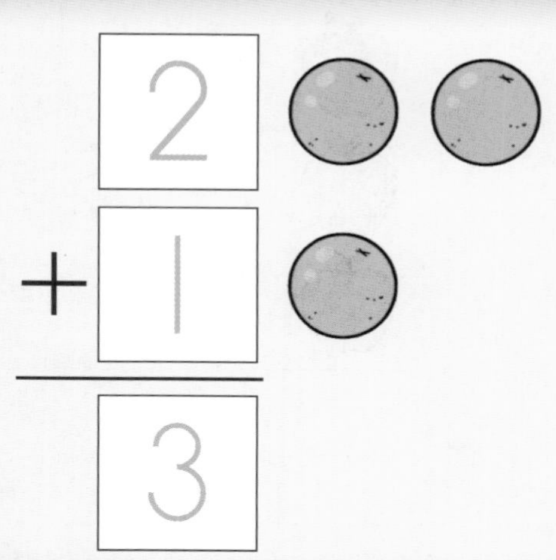

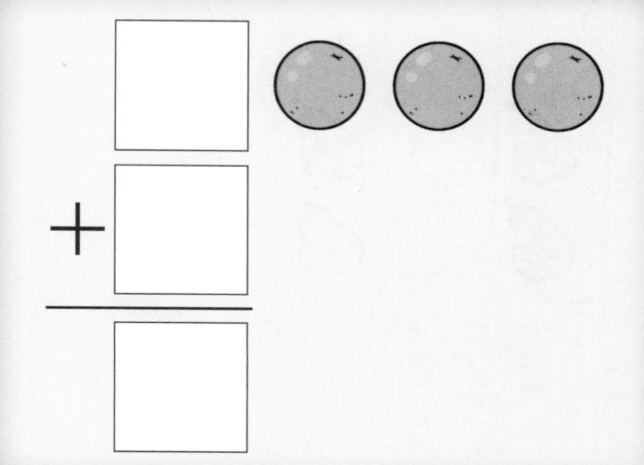

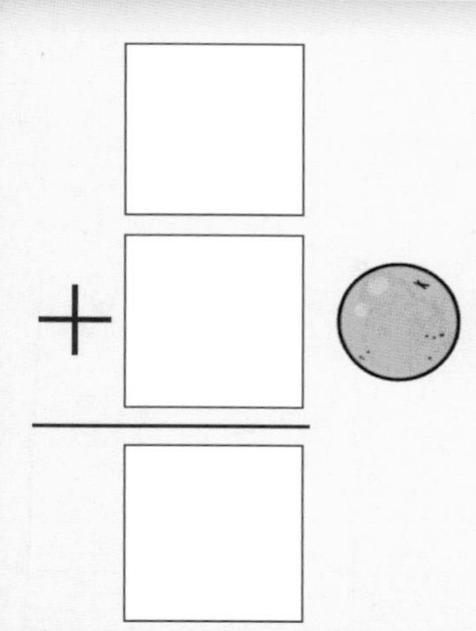

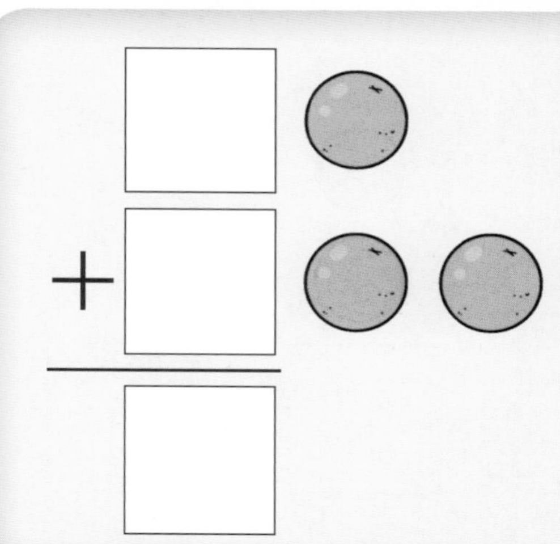

$$\begin{array}{r} 1 \\ +\ 1 \\ \hline \square \end{array} \qquad \begin{array}{r} 2 \\ +\ 1 \\ \hline \square \end{array} \qquad \begin{array}{r} 1 \\ +\ 2 \\ \hline \square \end{array} \qquad \begin{array}{r} 3 \\ +\ 0 \\ \hline \square \end{array}$$

Add

Add the numbers.

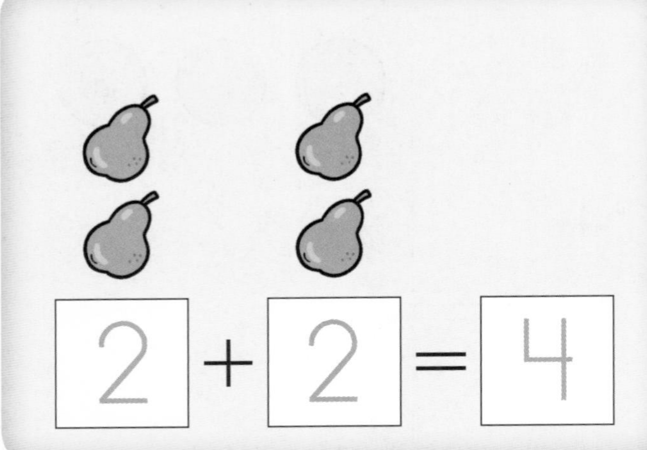

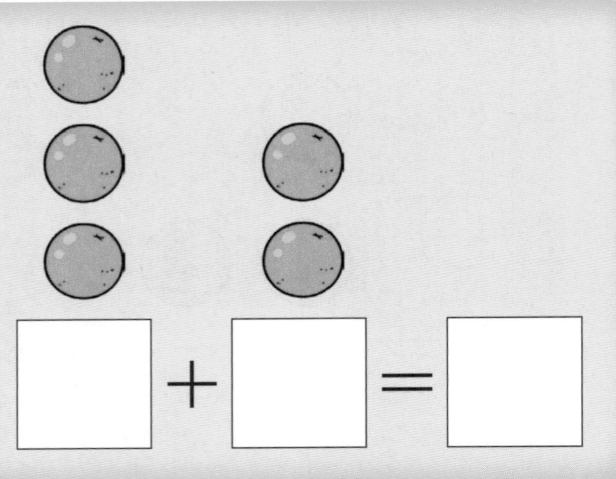

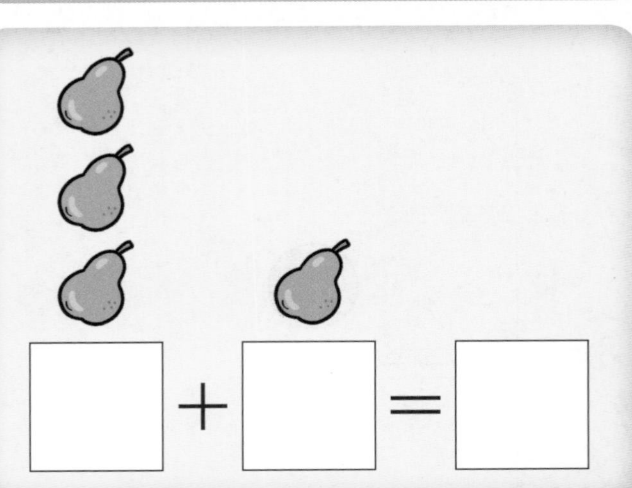

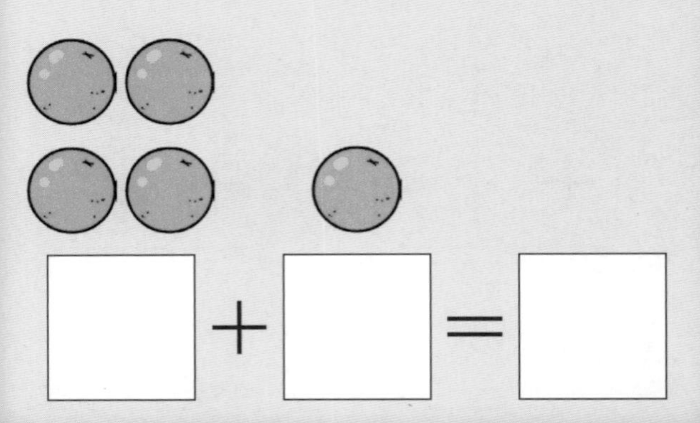

Add the numbers.

2
+ 2
4

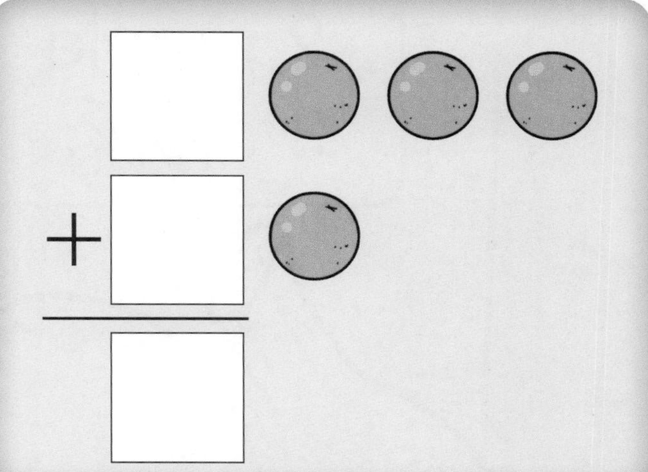

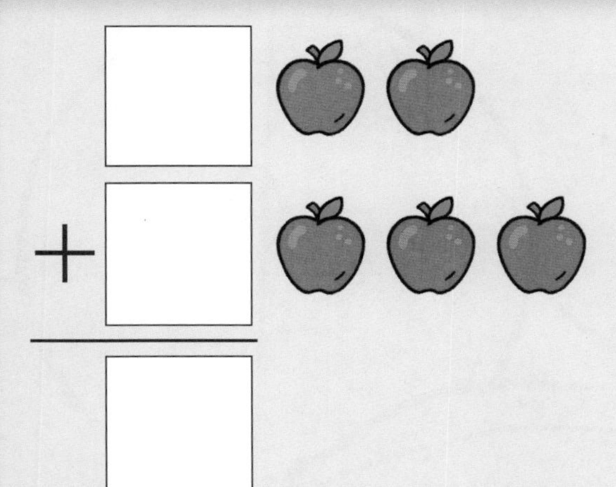

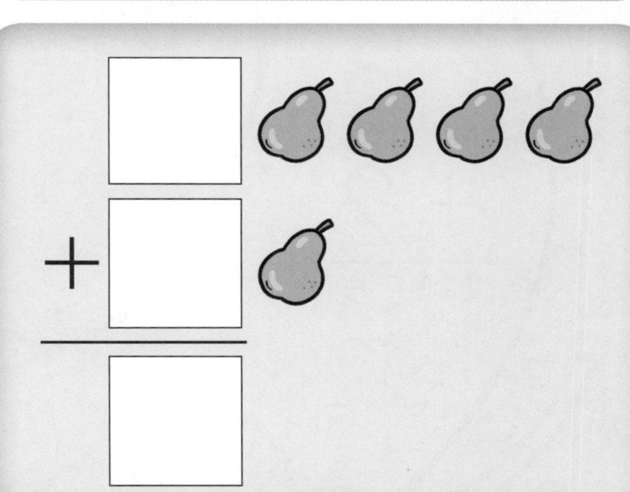

$$\begin{array}{r} 2 \\ +\,2 \\ \hline \end{array} \qquad \begin{array}{r} 3 \\ +\,1 \\ \hline \end{array} \qquad \begin{array}{r} 2 \\ +\,3 \\ \hline \end{array} \qquad \begin{array}{r} 4 \\ +\,1 \\ \hline \end{array}$$

Fruit Fun

Add and color.

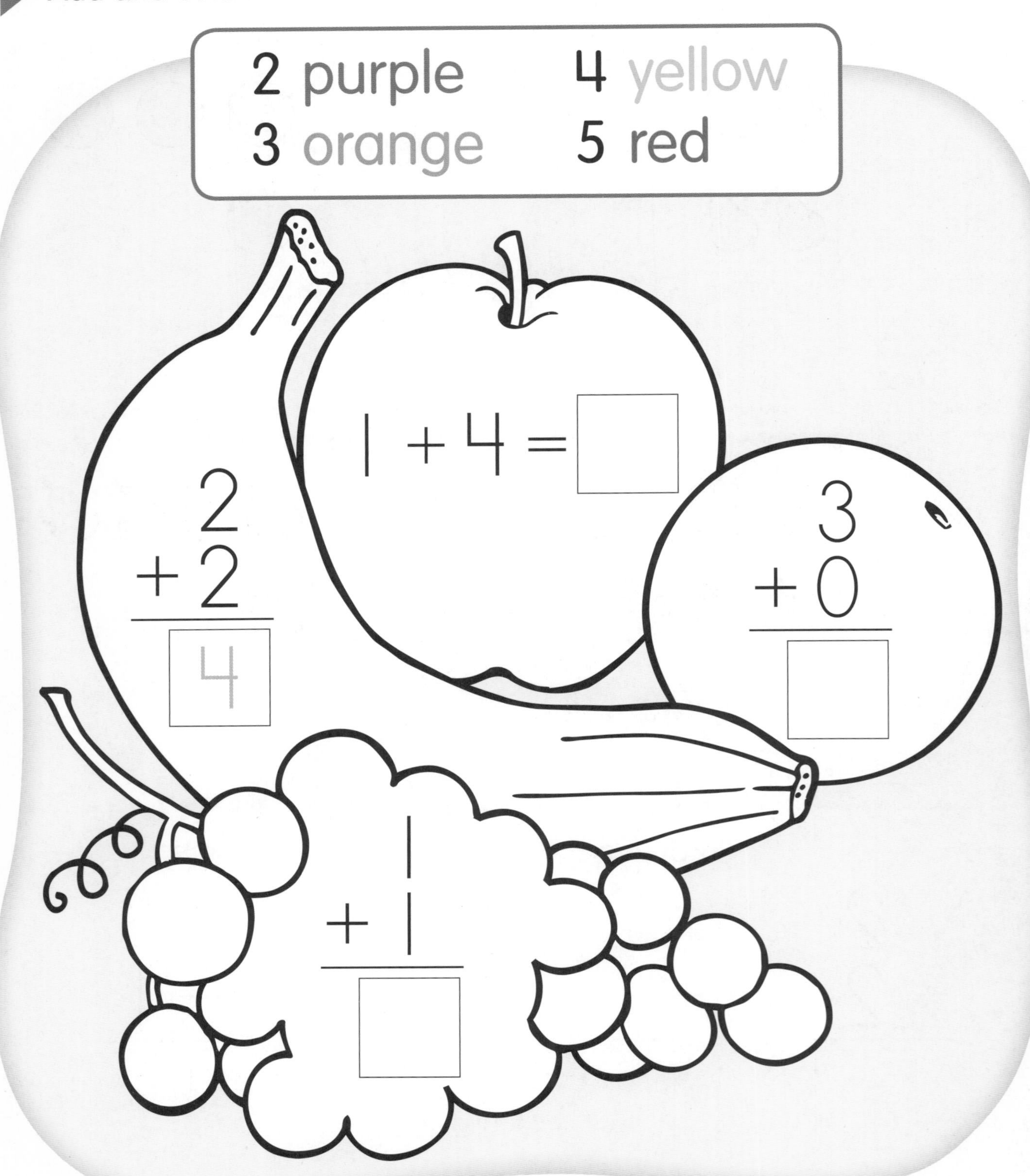

Hungry Squirrel

Help the squirrel find the tree.
Add. Connect the dots.

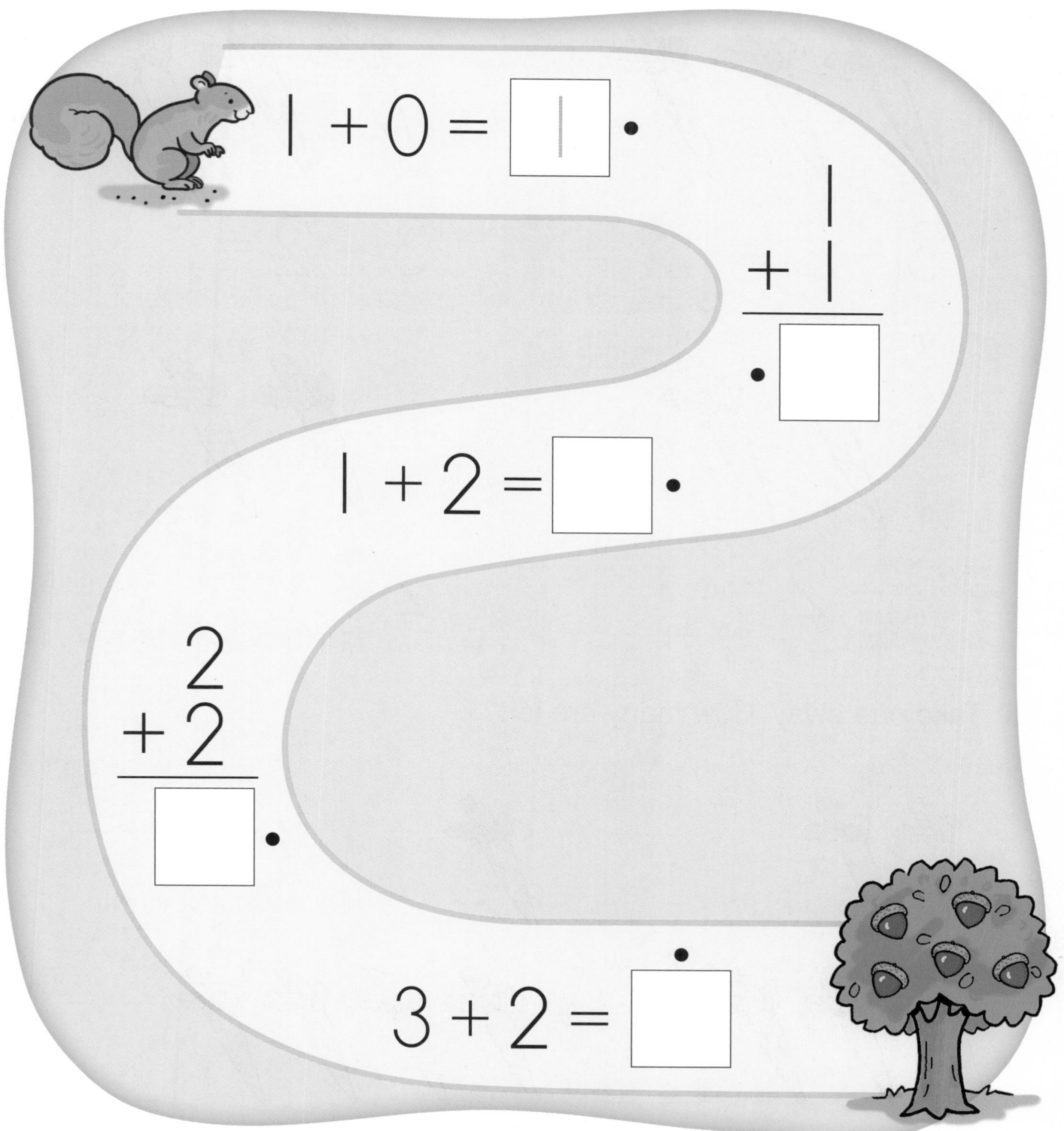

Subtract

How many are left?

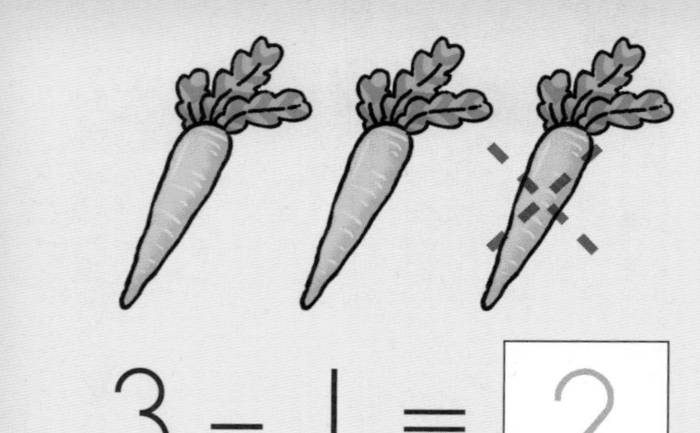

3 − 1 = 2

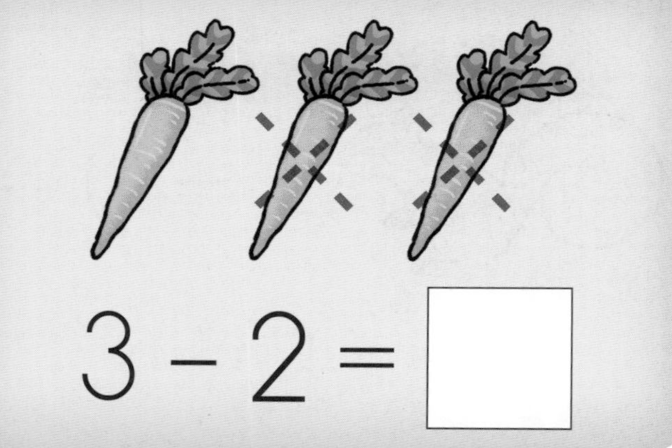

3 − 2 = ☐

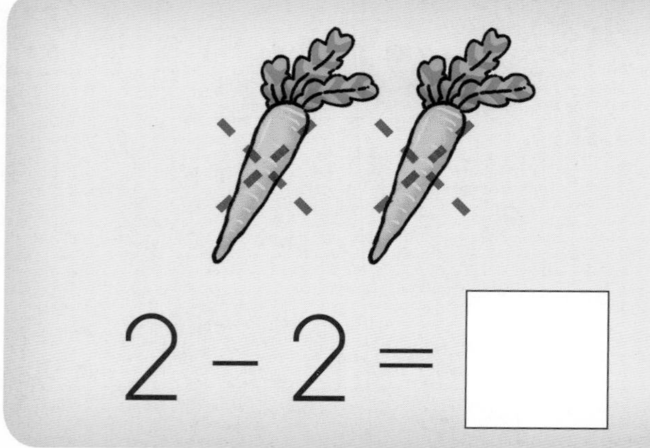

2 − 2 = ☐

2 − 1 = ☐

Take one away. How many are left?

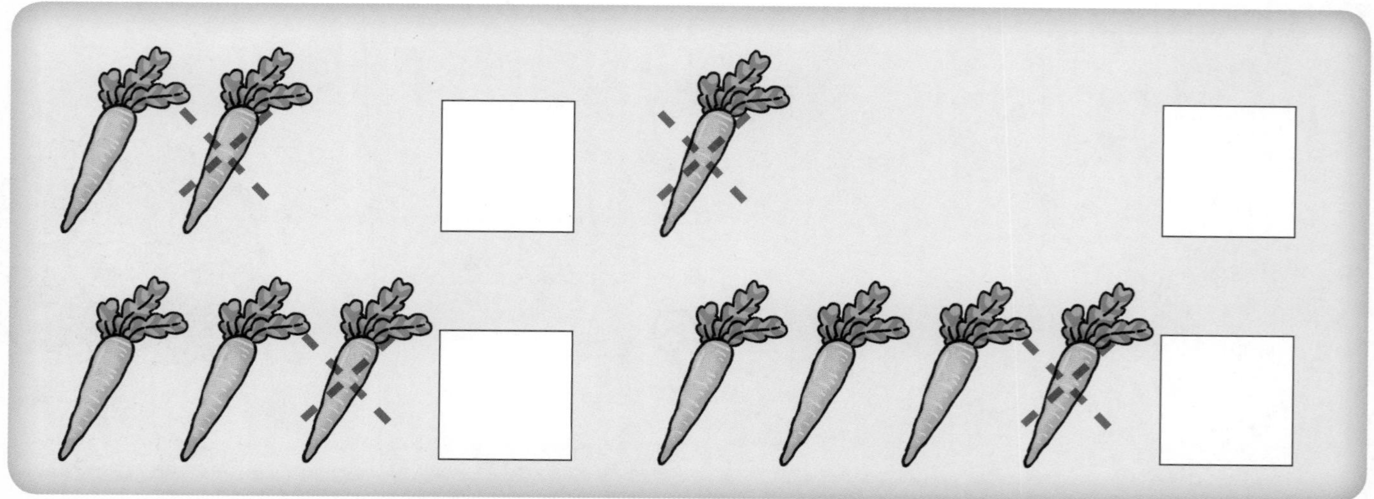

How many are left?

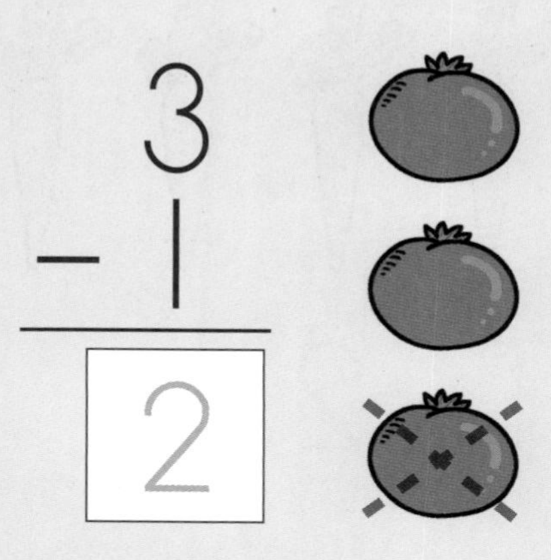

$$\begin{array}{r} 3 \\ -\ 1 \\ \hline 2 \end{array}$$

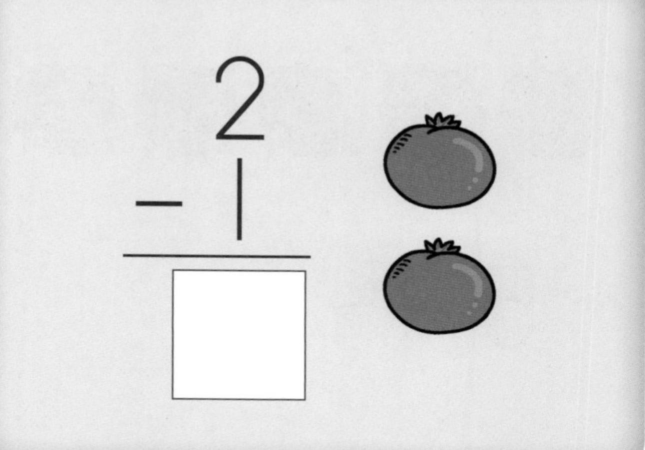

$$\begin{array}{r} 2 \\ -\ 1 \\ \hline \square \end{array}$$

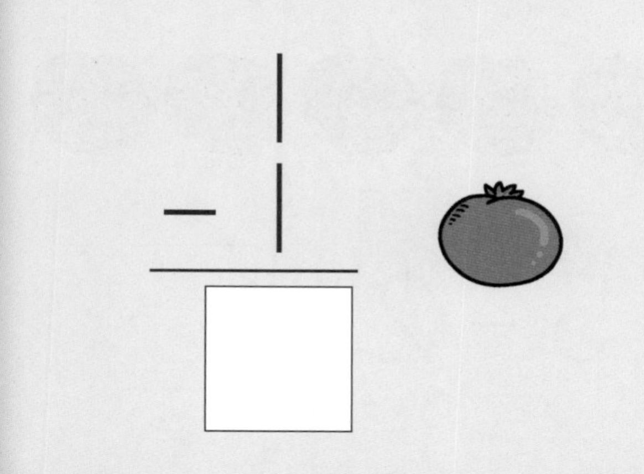

$$\begin{array}{r} 1 \\ -\ 1 \\ \hline \square \end{array}$$

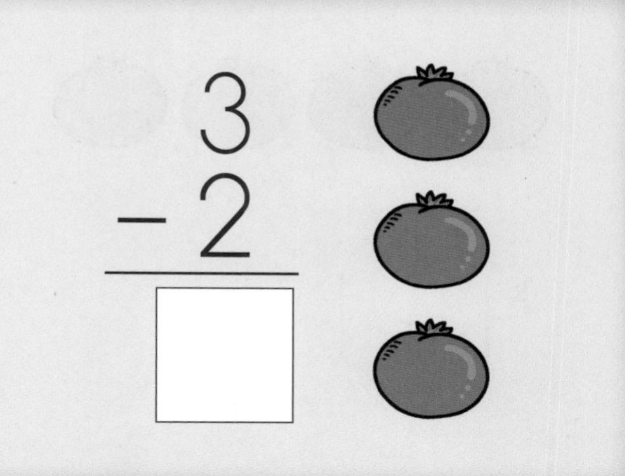

$$\begin{array}{r} 3 \\ -\ 2 \\ \hline \square \end{array}$$

$$\begin{array}{r} 2 \\ -\ 1 \\ \hline \square \end{array} \quad \begin{array}{r} 3 \\ -\ 2 \\ \hline \square \end{array} \quad \begin{array}{r} 1 \\ -\ 0 \\ \hline \square \end{array} \quad \begin{array}{r} 3 \\ -\ 1 \\ \hline \square \end{array}$$

Subtract

How many are left?

5 − 4 = 1

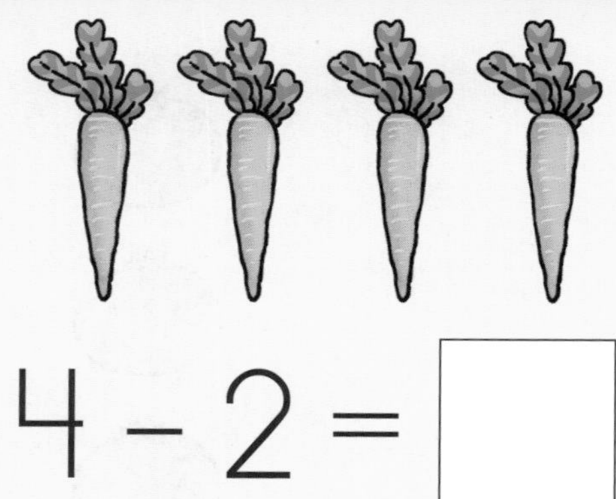

4 − 2 = ☐

4 − 1 = ☐

5 − 2 = ☐

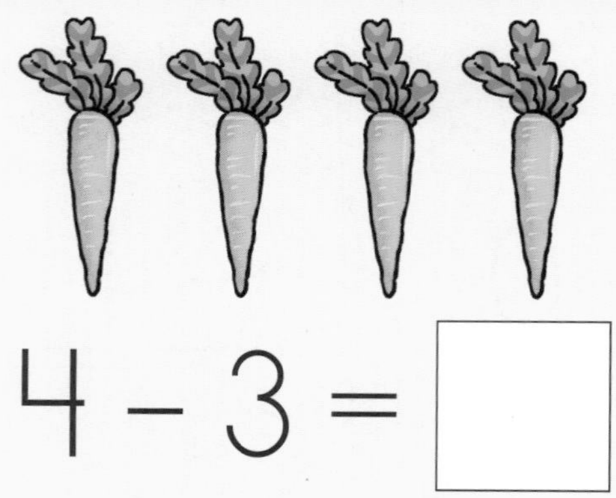

4 − 3 = ☐

5 − 3 = ☐

How many are left?

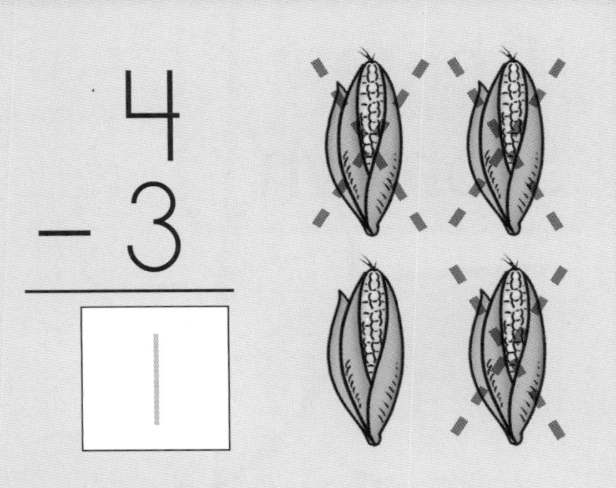

$$\begin{array}{r} 5 \\ -\ 1 \\ \hline \square \end{array}$$

$$\begin{array}{r} 5 \\ -\ 3 \\ \hline \square \end{array}$$

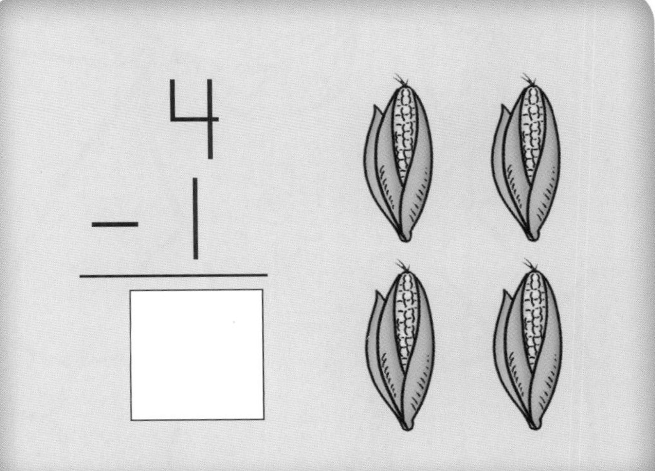

$$\begin{array}{r} 5 \\ -\ 1 \\ \hline \square \end{array} \qquad \begin{array}{r} 5 \\ -\ 3 \\ \hline \square \end{array} \qquad \begin{array}{r} 4 \\ -\ 3 \\ \hline \square \end{array} \qquad \begin{array}{r} 4 \\ -\ 1 \\ \hline \square \end{array}$$

In the Garden

Find the answers. Color.

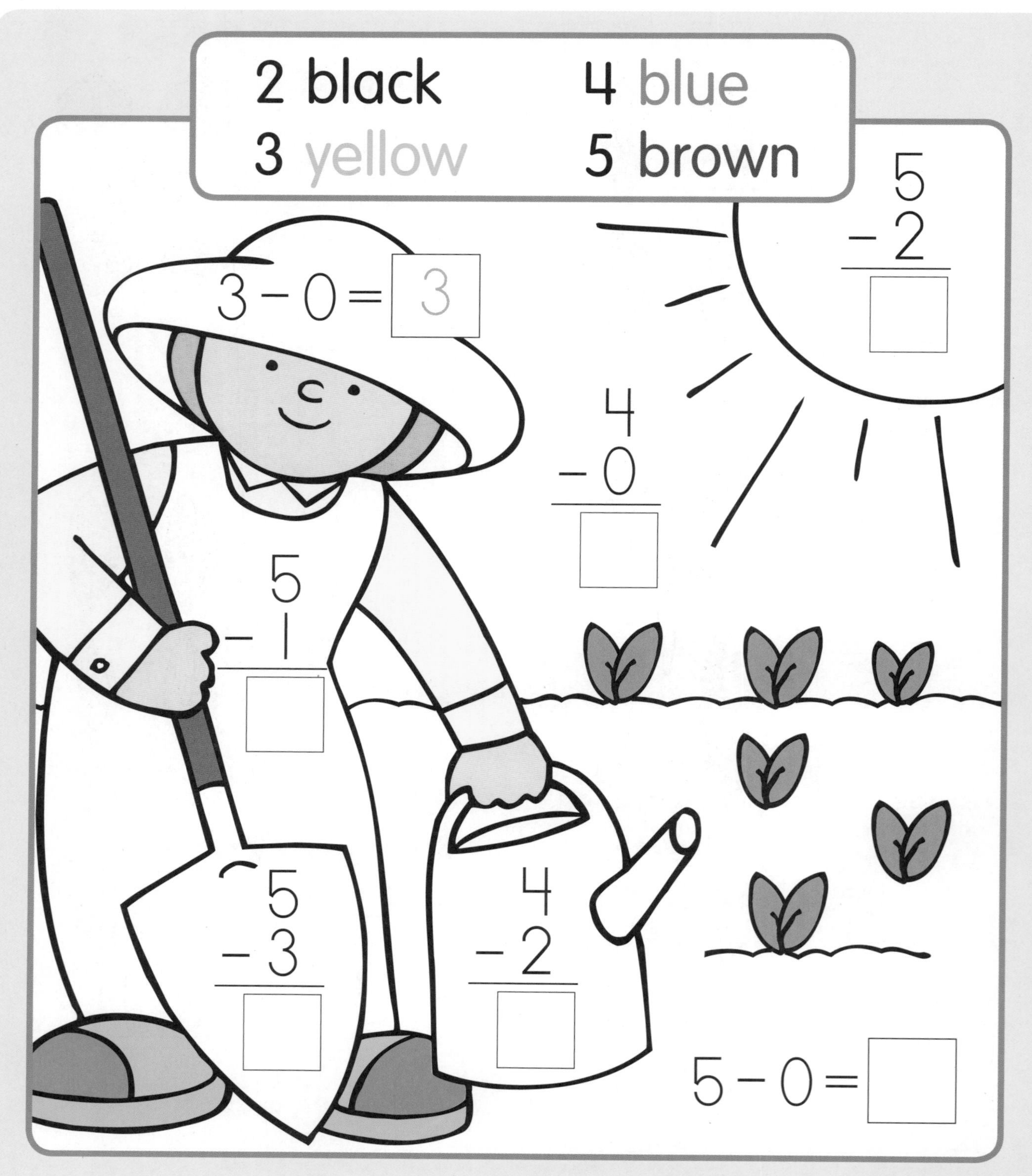

A Snack for Bunny

Find the answers.
Connect the dots. Start with **1**.

Add and Subtract

Find the answers.

$1 + 1 = \boxed{2}$ $2 - 1 = \square$

$0 + 3 = \square$ $3 - 0 = \square$

$1 + 2 = \square$ $3 - 2 = \square$

$2 + 1 = \square$ $3 - 1 = \square$

$$\begin{array}{r} 1 \\ +\,2 \\ \hline \square \end{array} \quad \begin{array}{r} 3 \\ -\,2 \\ \hline \square \end{array} \quad \begin{array}{r} 1 \\ +\,1 \\ \hline \square \end{array} \quad \begin{array}{r} 2 \\ -\,1 \\ \hline \square \end{array}$$

Find the answers.
Draw lines to match.

$2 + 1 =$ [3] •	• 0
$3 - 3 =$ [ ] •	• 1
$1 + 1 =$ [ ] •	• 2
$3 - 2 =$ [ ] •	• 3

Review to 5

Write the problems.

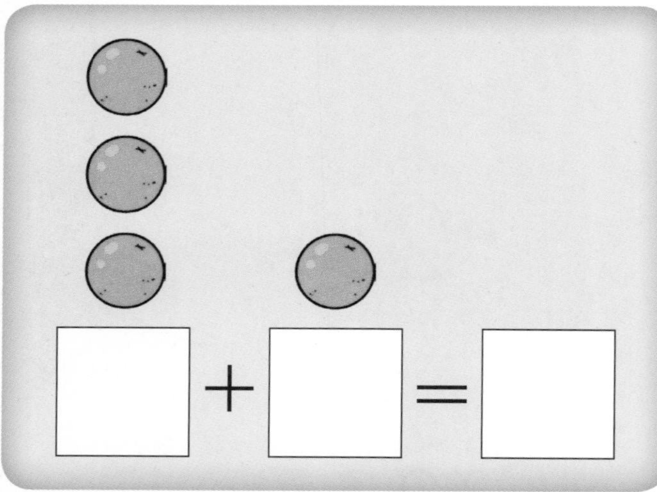

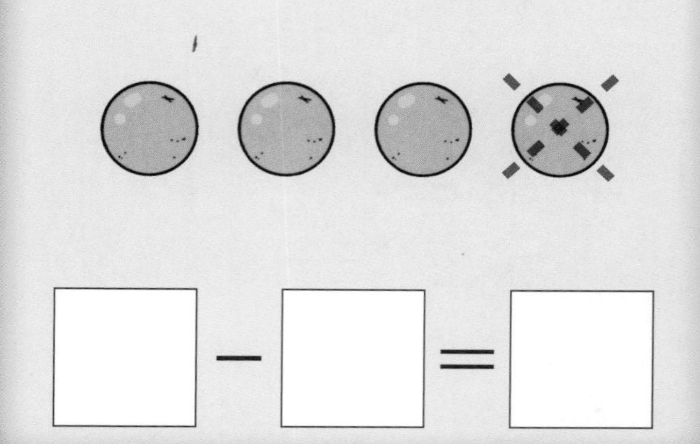

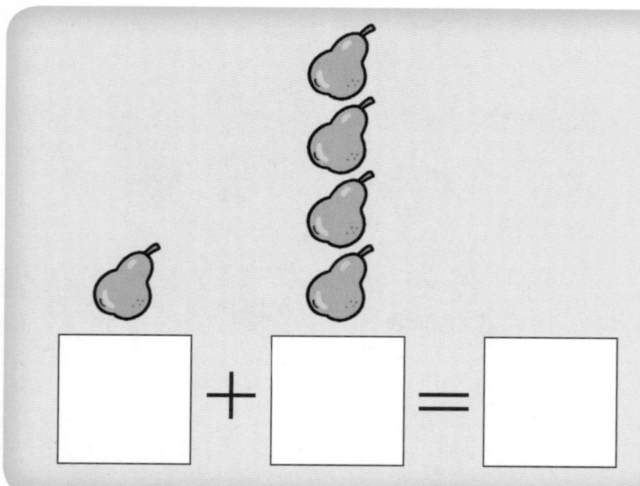

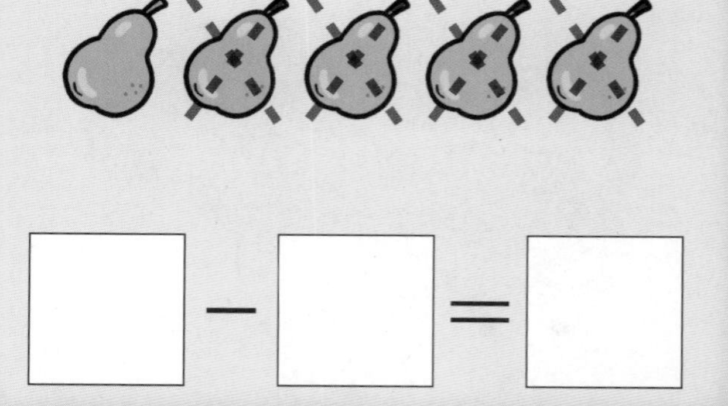

Write the problems.

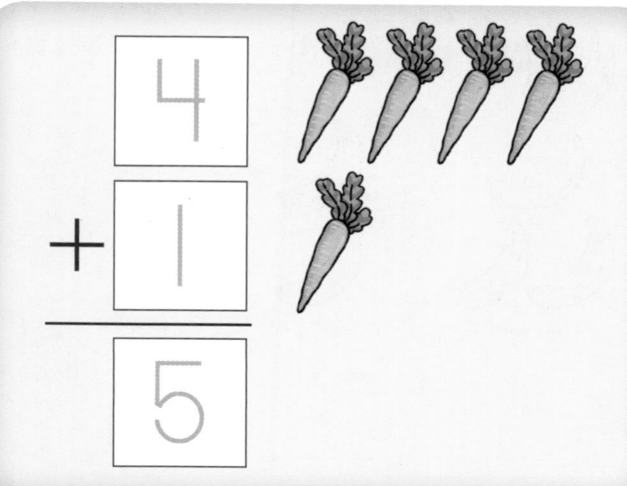

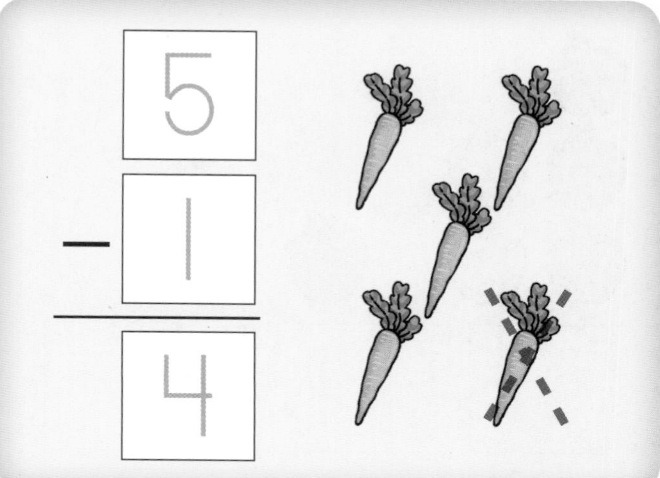

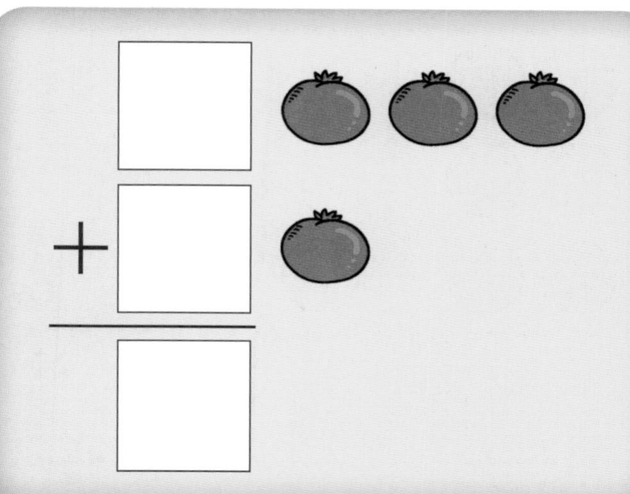

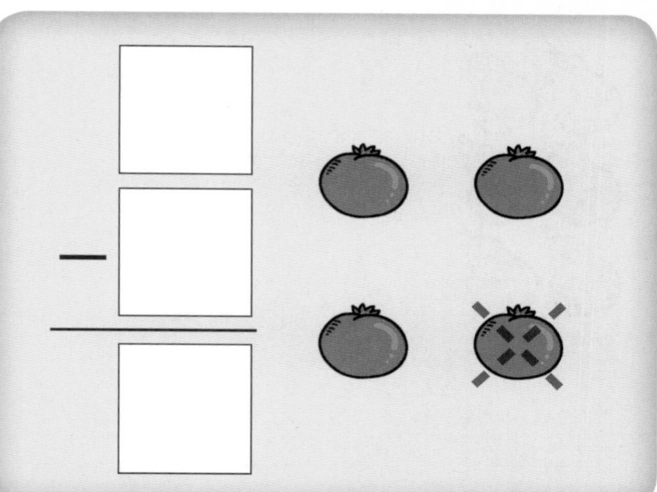

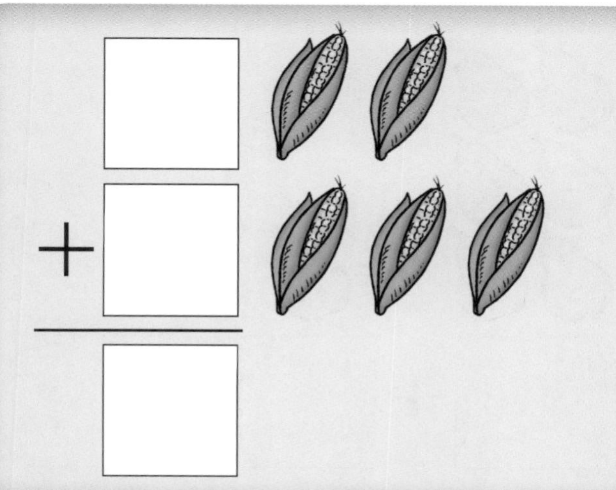

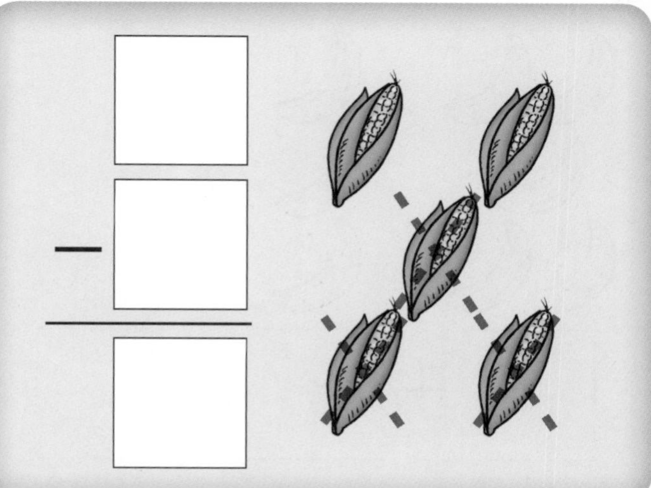

Add to 6, 7, 8

Write the problems.

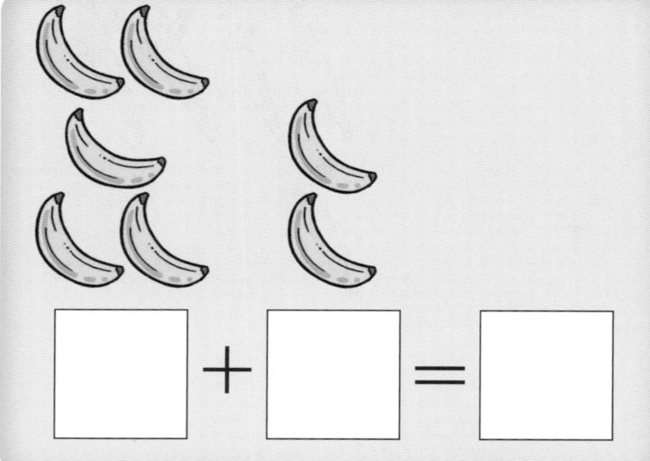

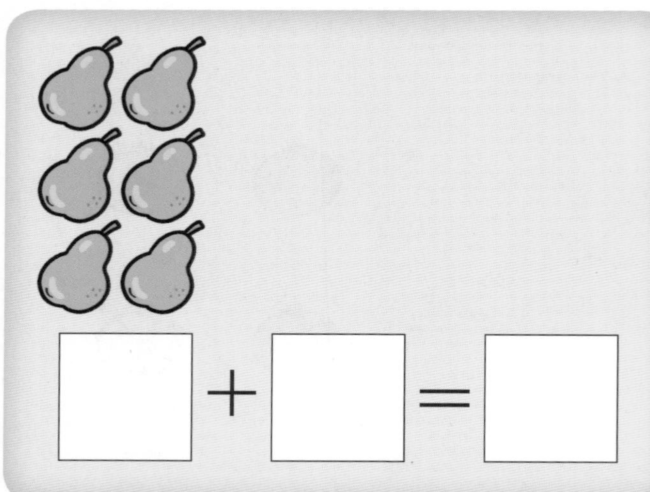

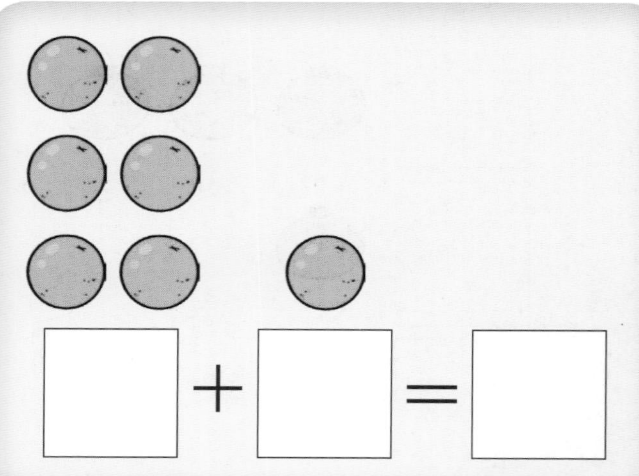

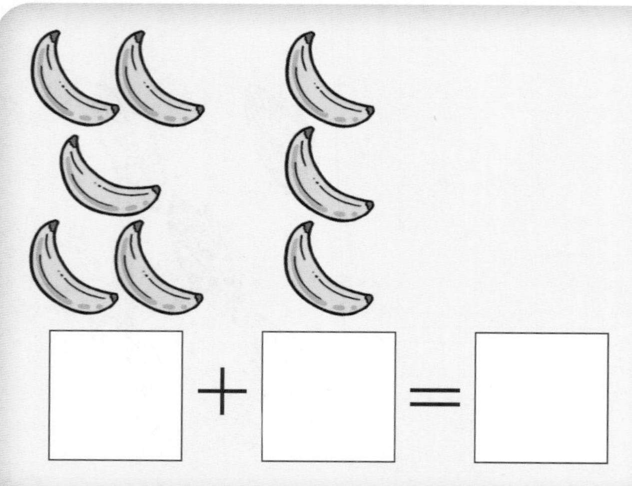

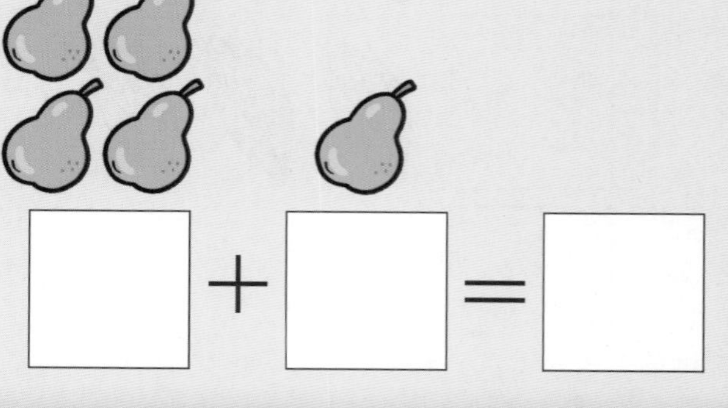

Write the problems.

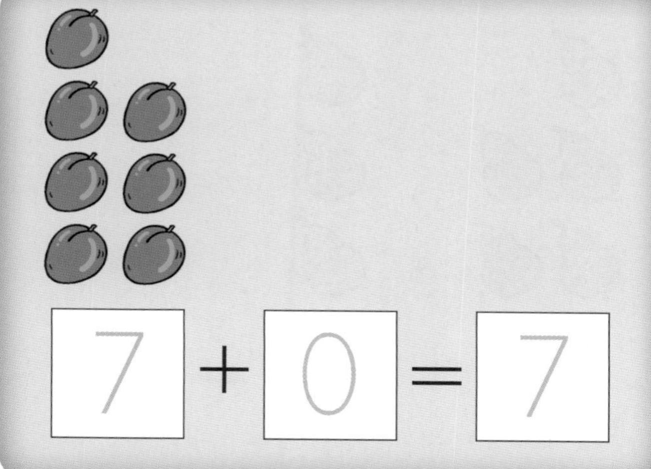

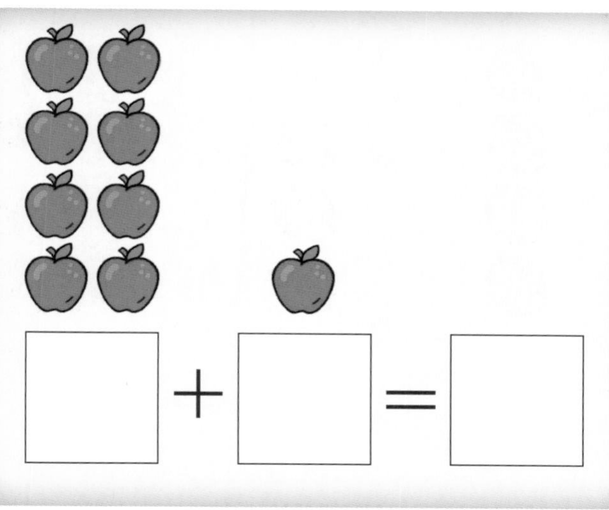

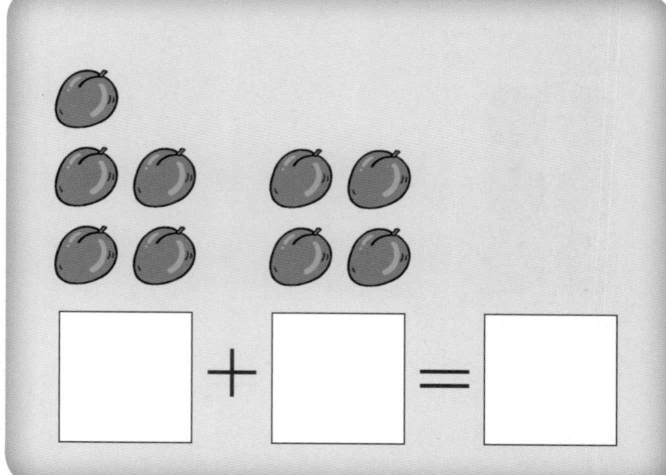

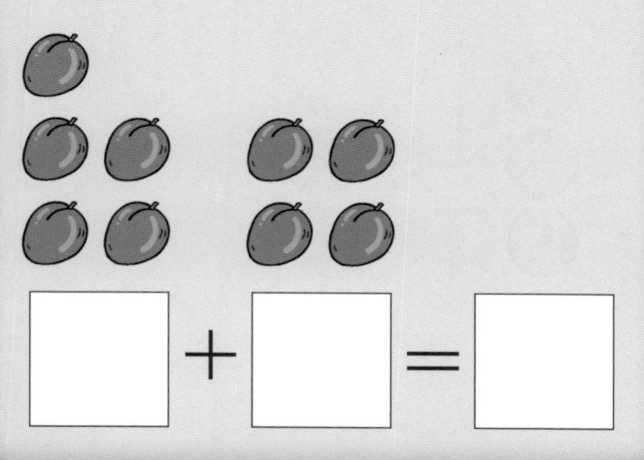

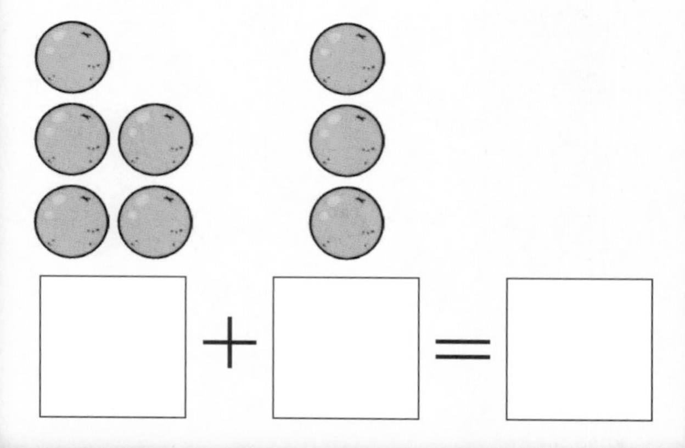

Add to 10

Write the problems.

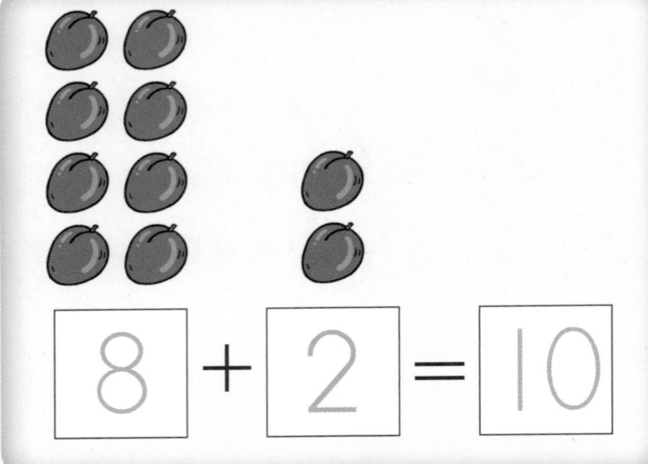

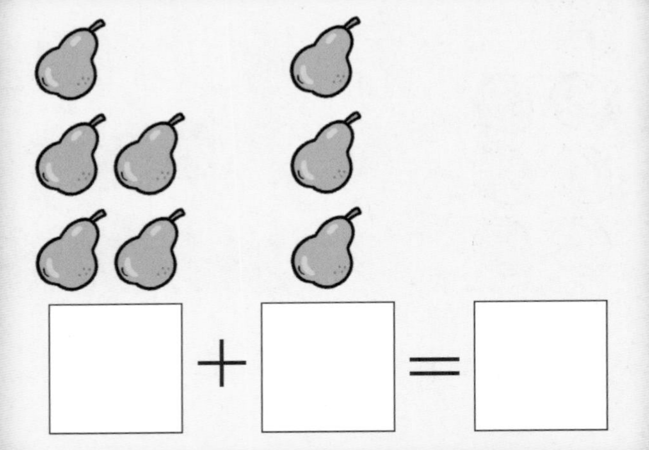

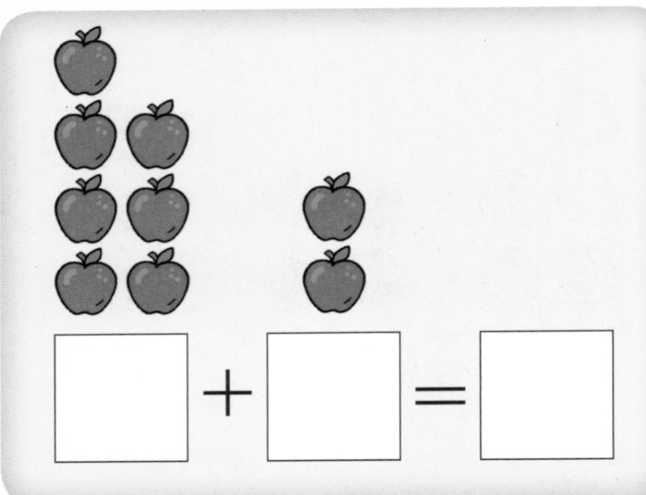

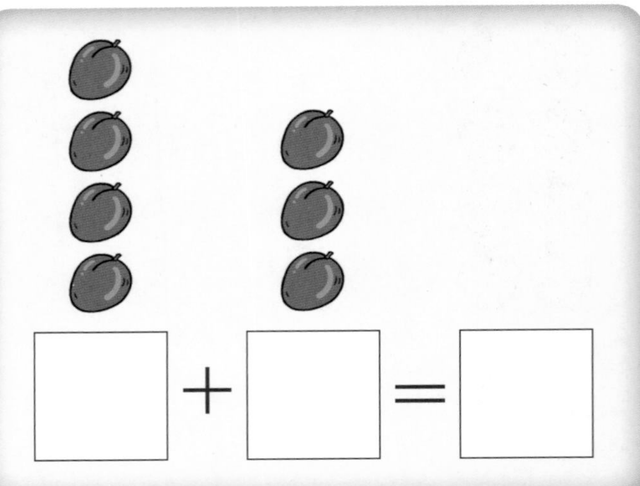

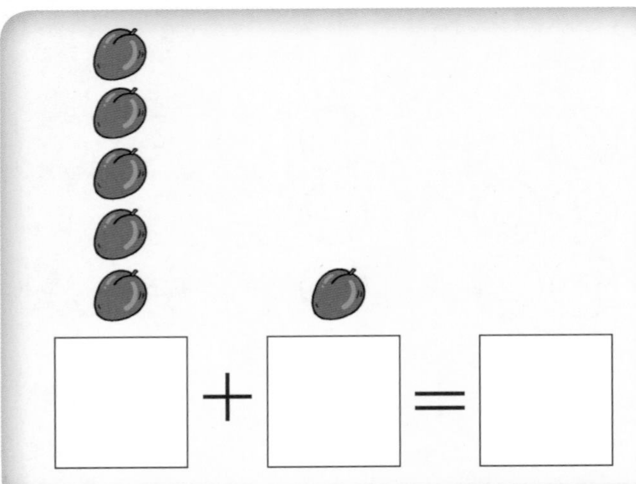

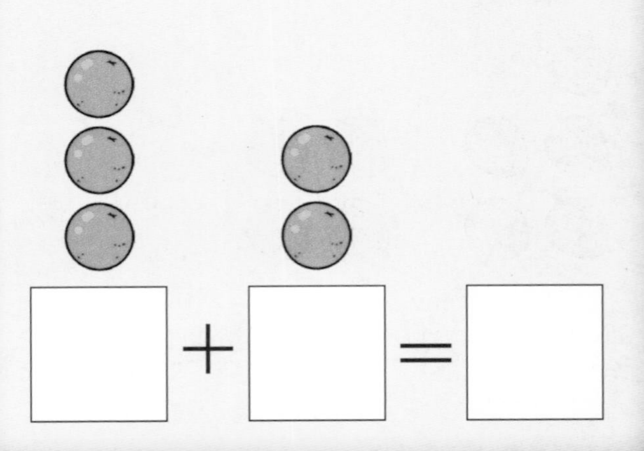

Apple Tree Addition

Find the answers. Color the picture.

$3+3=$ 6	red	$4+4=$ ☐	brown
$8+1=$ ☐	green	$5+2=$ ☐	yellow

Addition to 8, 9, 10

Add.

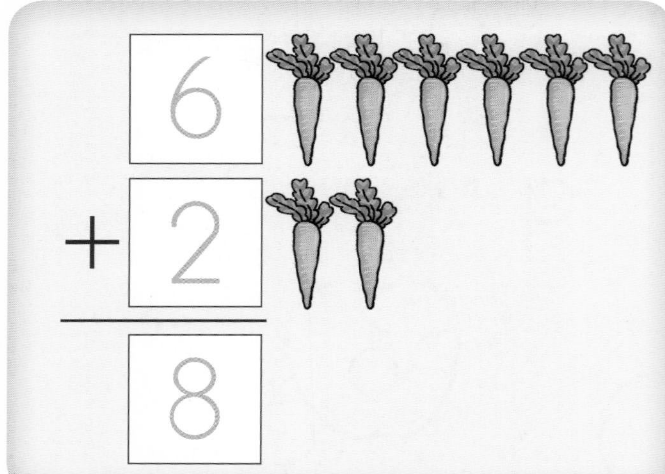

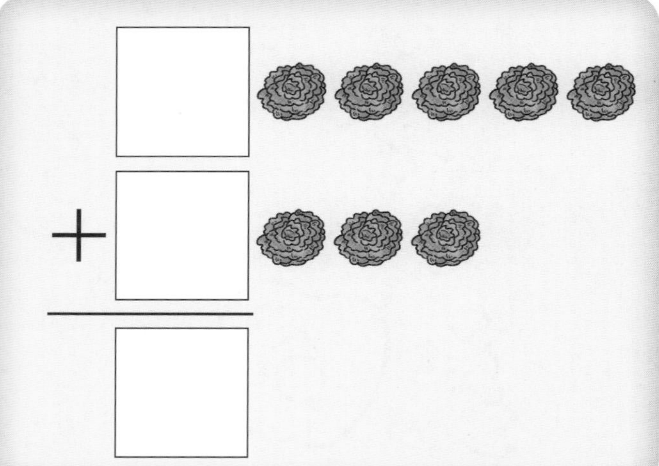

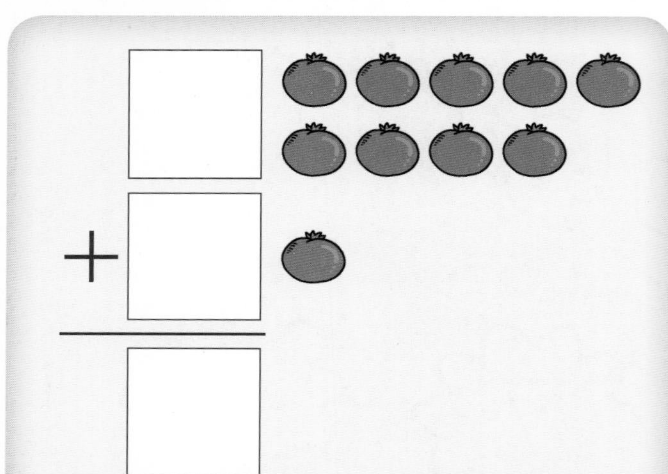

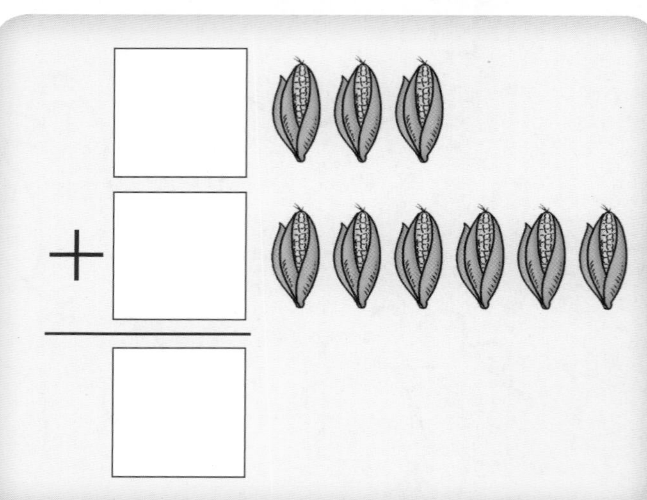

5	9	3	6
+ 3	+ 1	+ 6	+ 2
☐	☐	☐	☐

Picking Veggies

Add. Connect the dots. Start with **1**.

3 + 6 = ☐ •

8 + 0 = ☐ •

4 + 3 = ☐ •

3 + 3 = ☐ •

4 + 1 = ☐ •

2 + 2 = ☐ •

0 + 3 = ☐ •

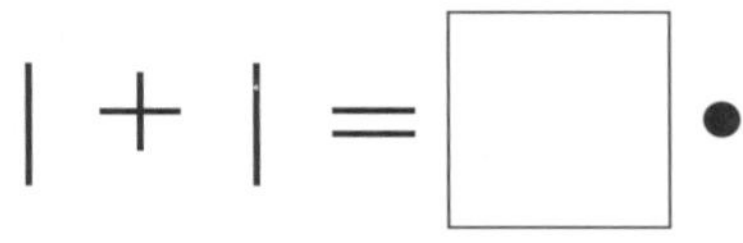

1 + 1 = ☐ •

$$\begin{array}{r} 1 \\ +\,0 \\ \hline 1 \end{array}$$ •

Subtract

How many are left?

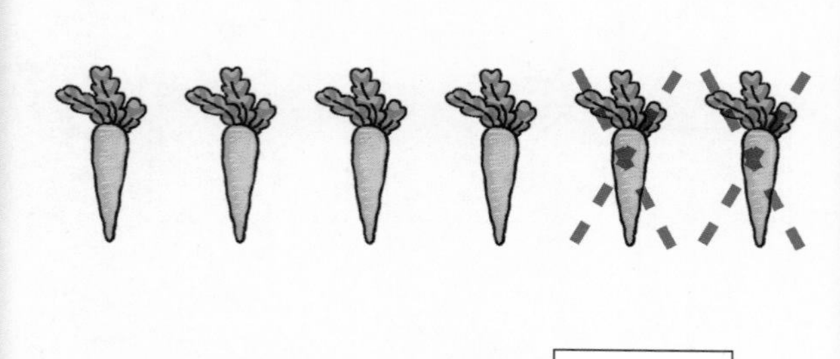

$6 - 2 = 4$

$7 - 3 = \square$

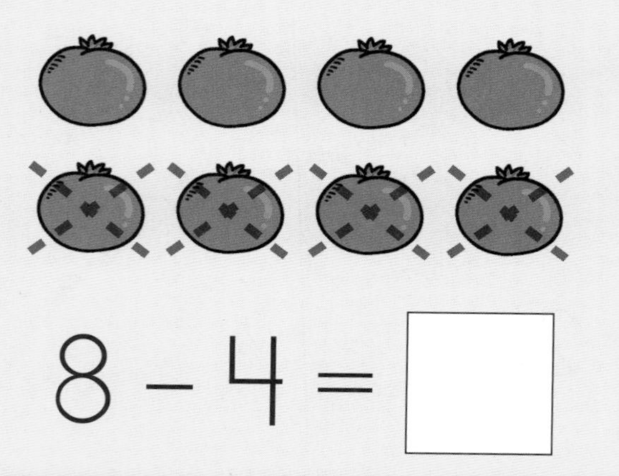

$8 - 4 = \square$

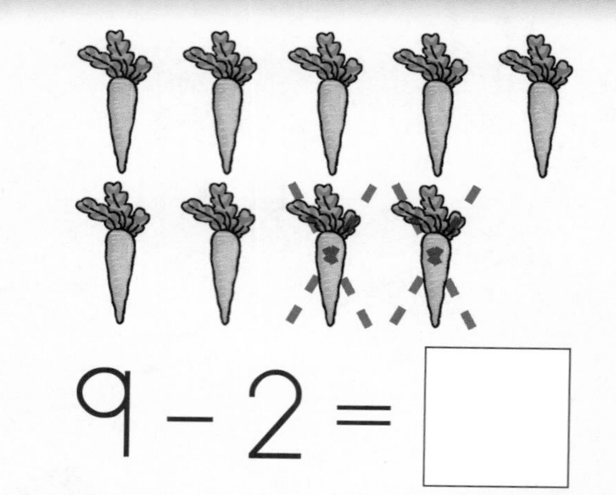

$9 - 2 = \square$

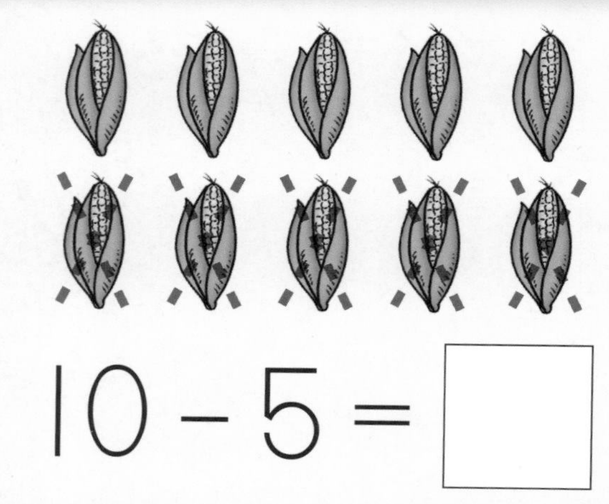

$10 - 5 = \square$

$7 - 2 = \square$

Funny Monkey

Find the answers. Color the picture.

6 – 3 =	3	brown	7 – 0 =		orange
8 – 2 =		red	10 – 5 =		yellow

Subtract

Find the answers.

7 − 4 = 3

9 − 3 = ☐

6 − 0 = ☐

8 − 2 = ☐

10 − 2 = ☐

9 − 5 = ☐

Subtract from 10

Find the answers.
Draw lines to match.

10 − 2 = 8 •	• 5
10 − 5 = ☐ •	• 6
10 − 4 = ☐ •	• 7
10 − 1 = ☐ •	• 8
10 − 0 = ☐ •	• 9
10 − 3 = ☐ •	• 10

Big and Red

Find the answers.
Connect the dots. Start with **1**. Then color.

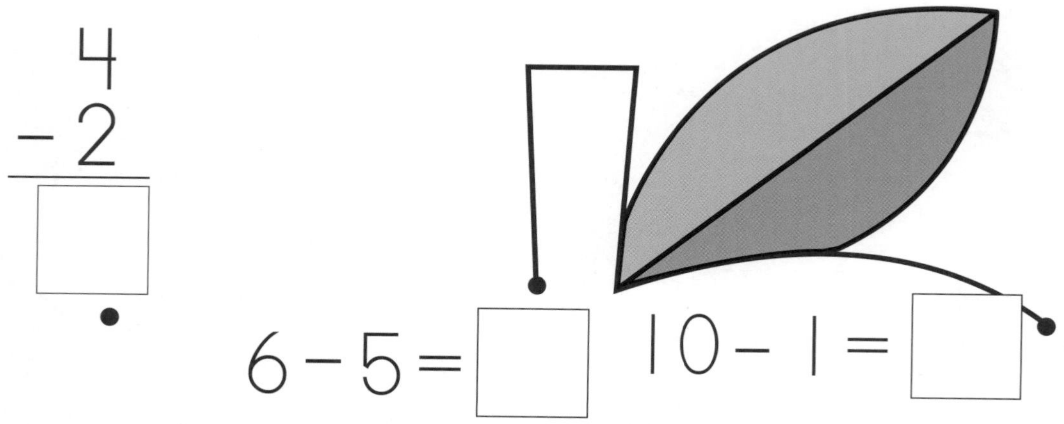

$$\begin{array}{r} 4 \\ -\ 2 \\ \hline \square \end{array}$$

$6 - 5 = \square$

$10 - 1 = \square$

$$\begin{array}{r} 5 \\ -\ 2 \\ \hline \square \end{array}$$

$9 - 1 = \square$

$$\begin{array}{r} 8 \\ -\ 4 \\ \hline \square \end{array}$$

$$\begin{array}{r} 8 \\ -\ 1 \\ \hline \square \end{array}$$

$$\begin{array}{r} 10 \\ -\ 5 \\ \hline \square \end{array}$$

$$\begin{array}{r} 6 \\ -\ 0 \\ \hline \square \end{array}$$

Find the answers.

$1 + 1 = \square$

$2 - 1 = \square$

$2 + 2 = \square$

$4 - 2 = \square$

$3 + 3 = \square$

$6 - 3 = \square$

$4 + 4 = \square$

$8 - 4 = \square$

$5 + 5 = \square$

$10 - 5 = \square$

Review to 10

Find the answers.

$5 + 1 = \square$

$6 - 1 = \square$

$6 + 1 = \square$

$7 - 1 = \square$

$7 + 1 = \square$

$8 - 1 = \square$

$8 + 1 = \square$

$9 - 1 = \square$

$9 + 1 = \square$

$10 - 1 = \square$

Answer Key

Please take time to go over the work your child has completed. Ask your child to explain what he or she has done. Praise both success and effort. If mistakes have been made, explain what the answer should have been and how to find it. Let your child know that mistakes are a part of learning. The time you spend with your child helps let him or her know you feel learning is important.

Page 2

Counting 1–10
Help the ant get to the sugar.
Color the numbers in order. Start with 1.

Page 3

Page 4

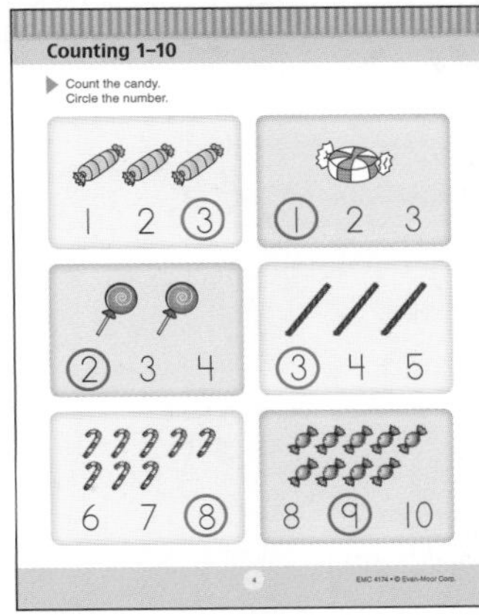

Counting 1–10
Count the candy.
Circle the number.

Page 5

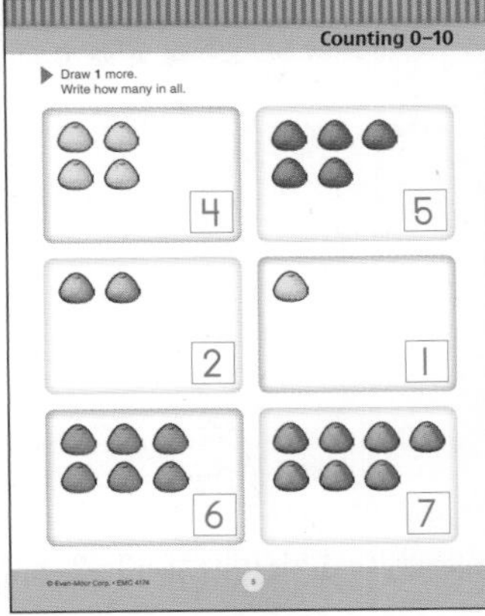

Page 6

Page 7

Counting 1–12
Help Max get to the doughnuts.
Write the missing numbers.
12 is 1 dozen. Draw an X on 1 dozen doughnuts.

Page 8

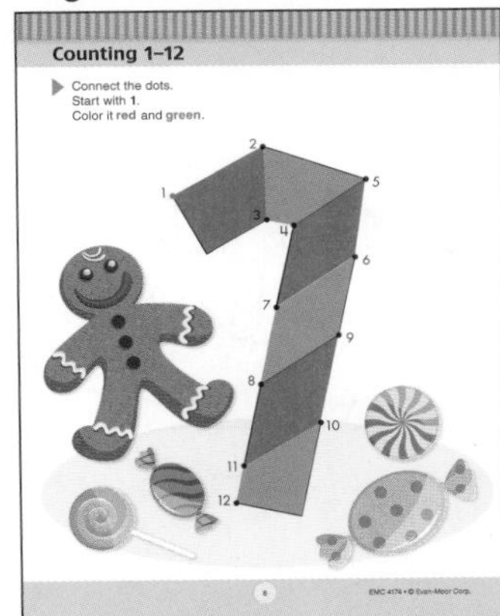

Page 9

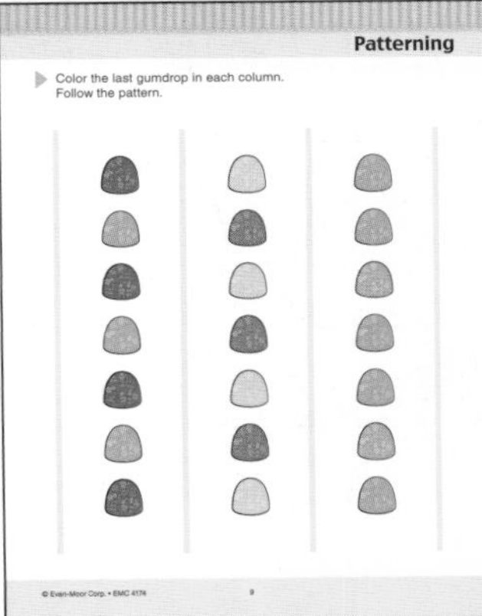

Patterning
Color the last gumdrop in each column.
Follow the pattern.

Page 10

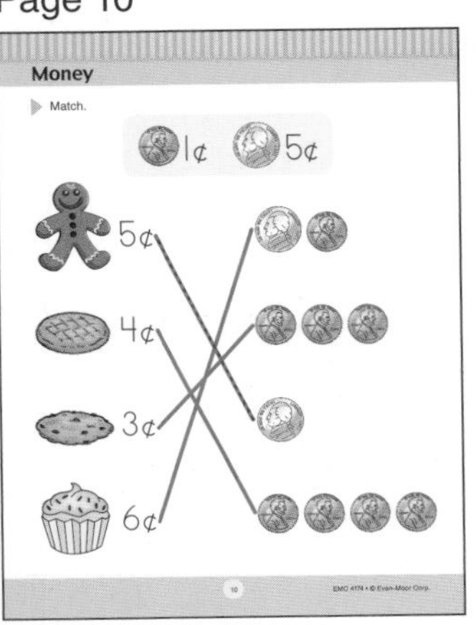

Page 11

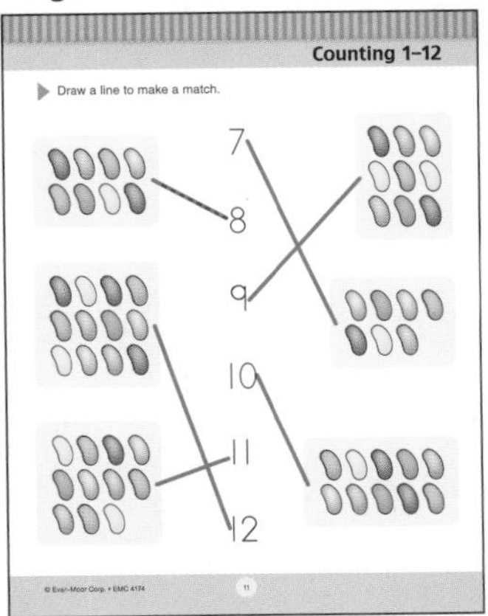

Counting 1–12
Draw a line to make a match.

Page 12

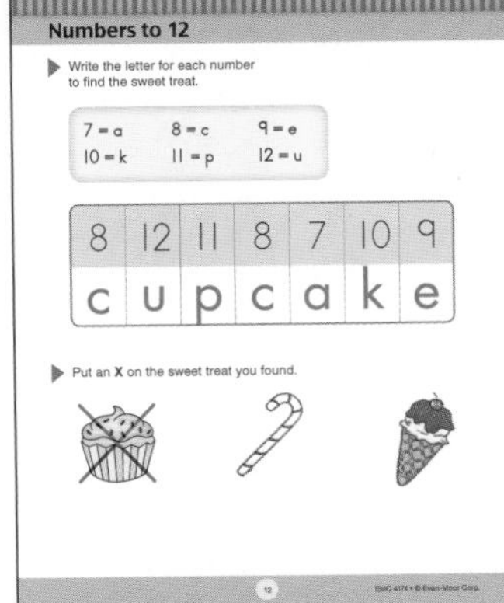

Page 13

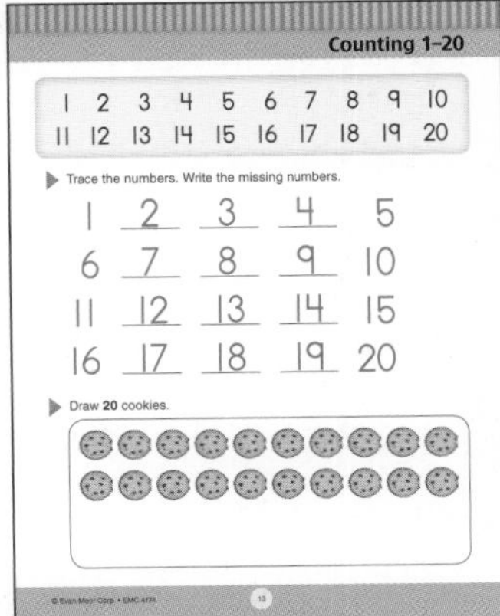

Counting 1–20
Trace the numbers. Write the missing numbers.
Draw 20 cookies.

Page 14

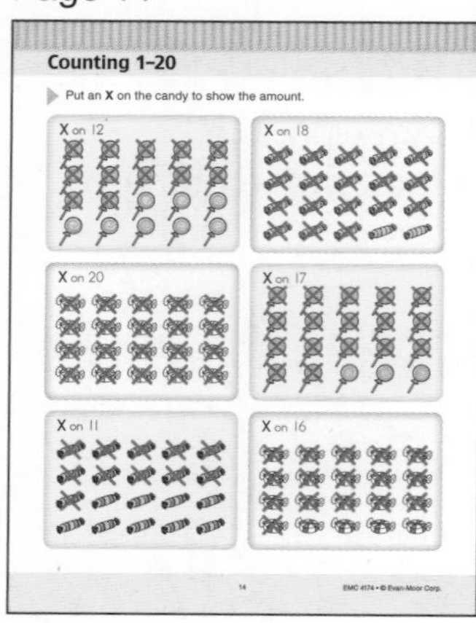

Counting 1–20
Put an X on the candy to show the amount.
X on 12
X on 18
X on 20
X on 17
X on 11
X on 16

Page 15

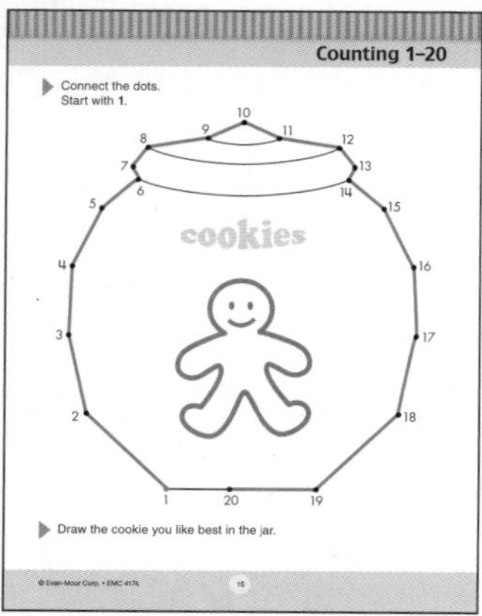

Counting 1–20
Connect the dots.
Start with 1.
cookies
Draw the cookie you like best in the jar.

Page 16

Counting 1–25
Help Josh get to the bakery. Write the missing numbers. Count to 25.
1 2 3 4
5
10 9 8 7 6
11 12 13 14 15
16
20 19 18 17
21
22 23 24 25
Bakery

Page 17

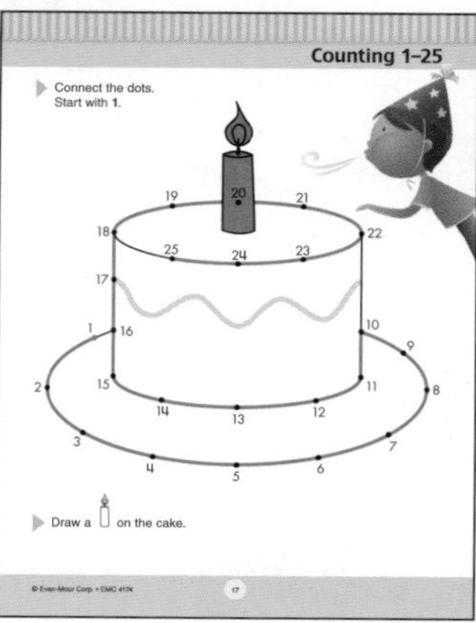

Counting 1–25
Connect the dots.
Start with 1.
on the cake.

Page 18

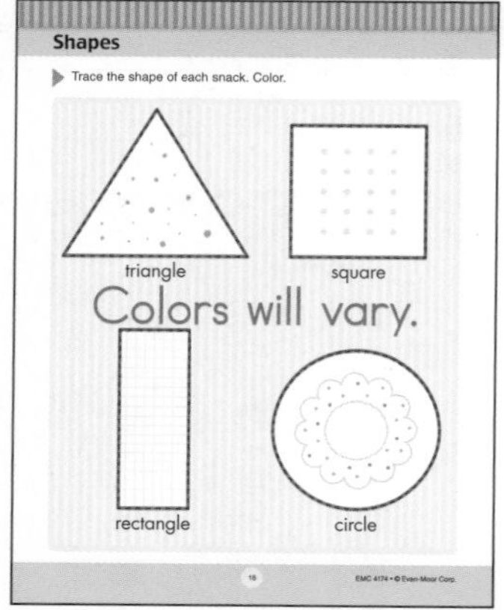

Page 19

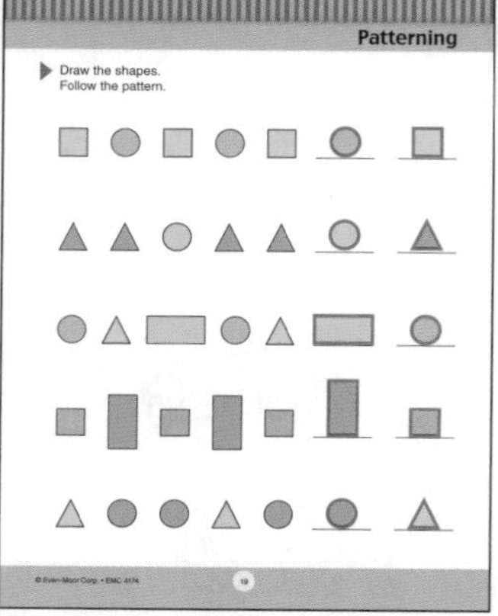

Page 20

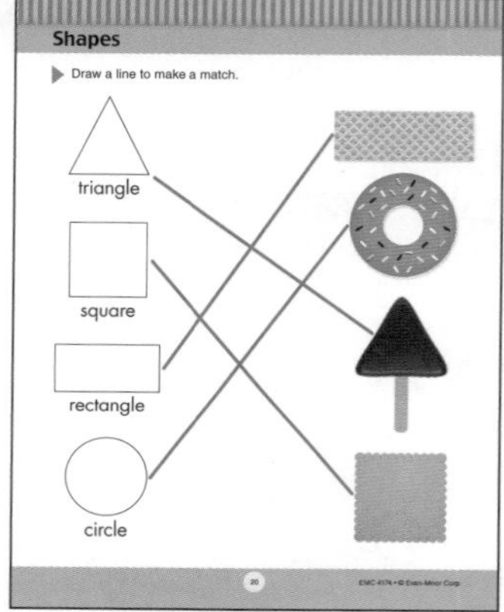

Page 21

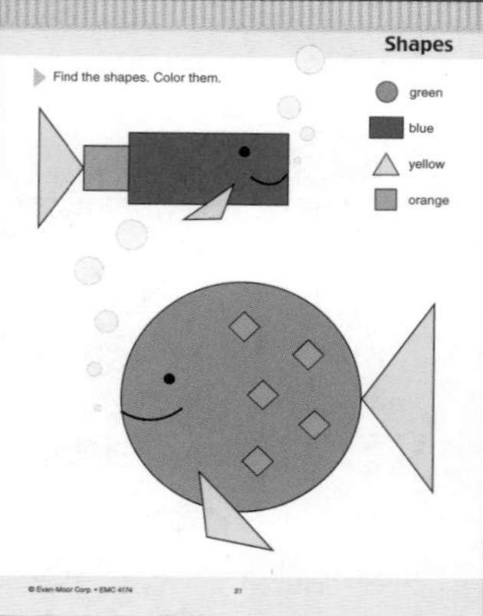

Page 22

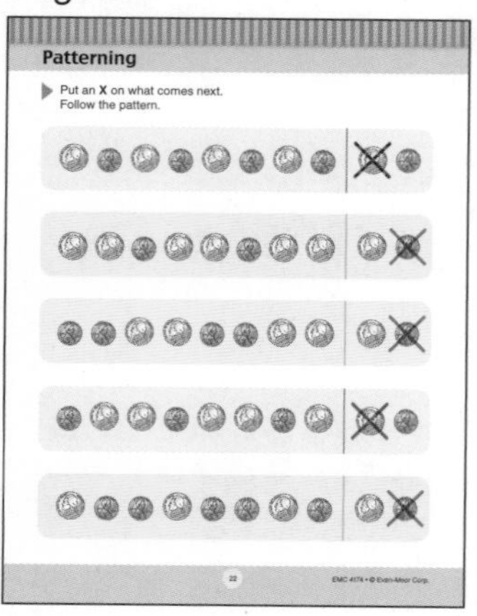

Patterning
Put an X on what comes next.
Follow the pattern.

Page 23

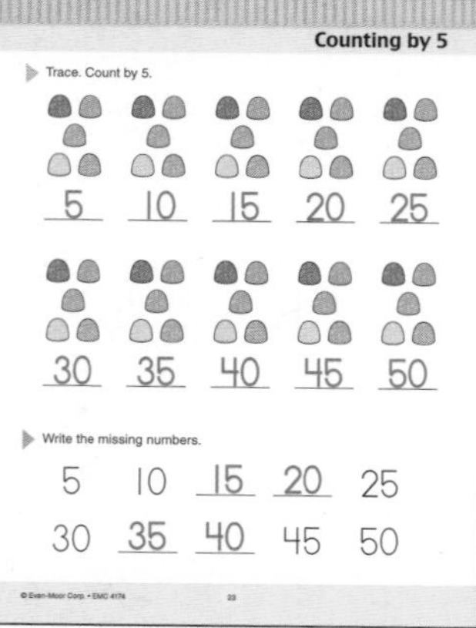

Counting by 5
Trace. Count by 5.
5 10 15 20 25
30 35 40 45 50
Write the missing numbers.
5 10 15 20 25
30 35 40 45 50

Page 24

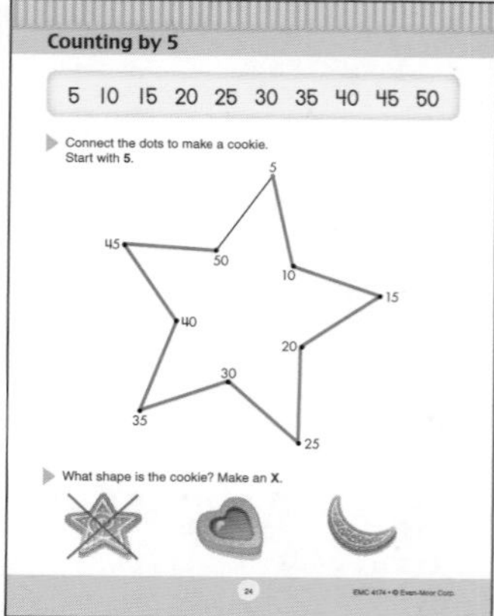

Counting by 5
5 10 15 20 25 30 35 40 45 50
Connect the dots to make a cookie.
Start with 5.
What shape is the cookie? Make an X.

Page 25

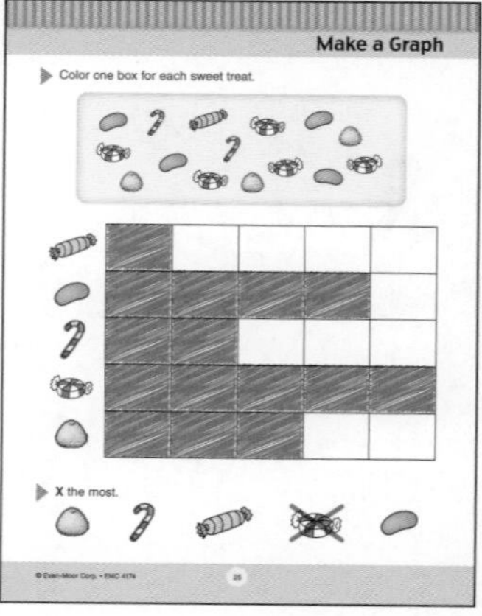

Make a Graph
Color one box for each sweet treat.
X the most.

Page 26

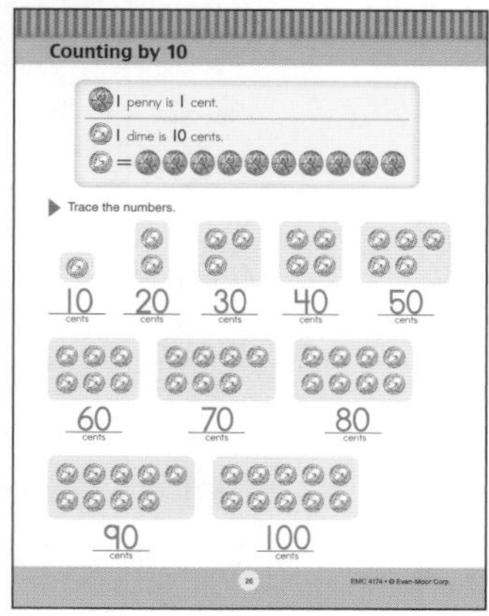

Page 27

Page 28

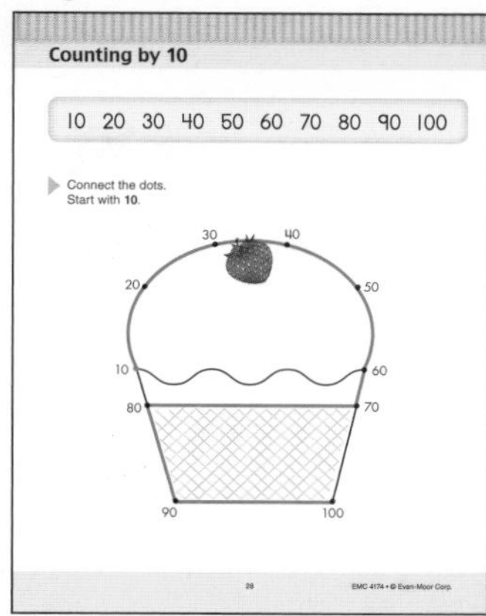

Page 29

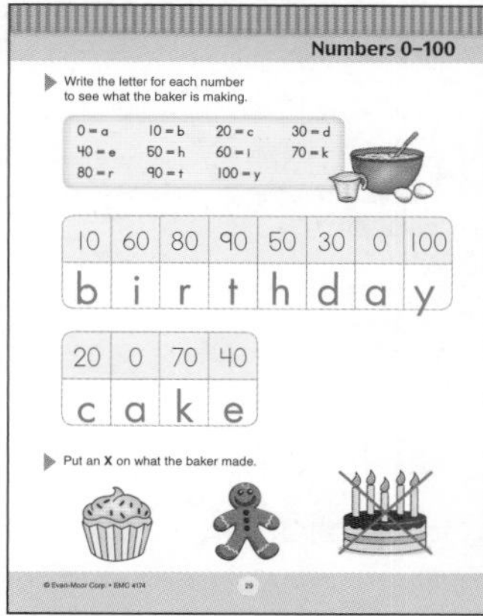

Page 30

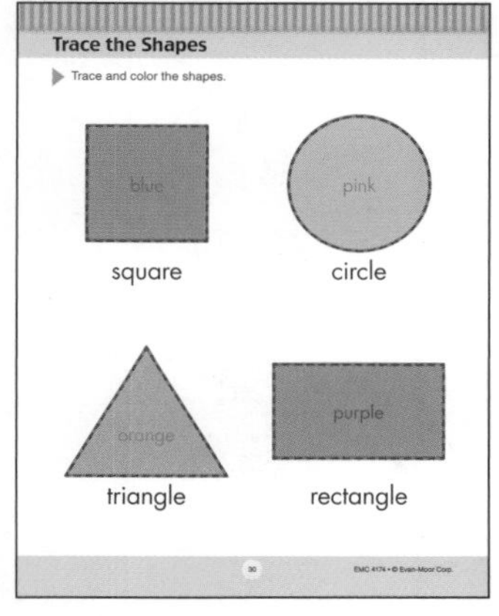

Page 31

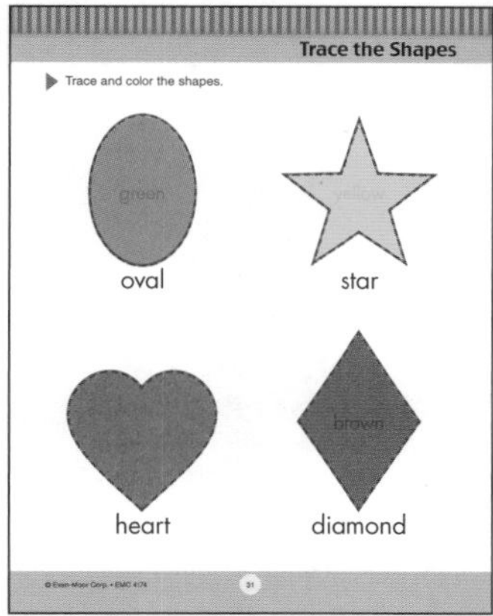

Page 32

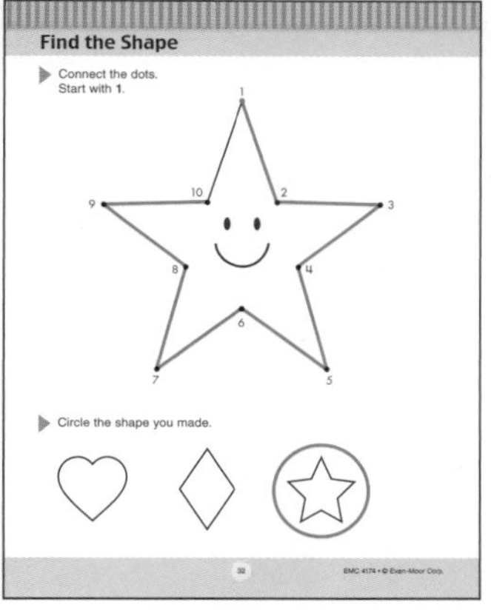

Page 33

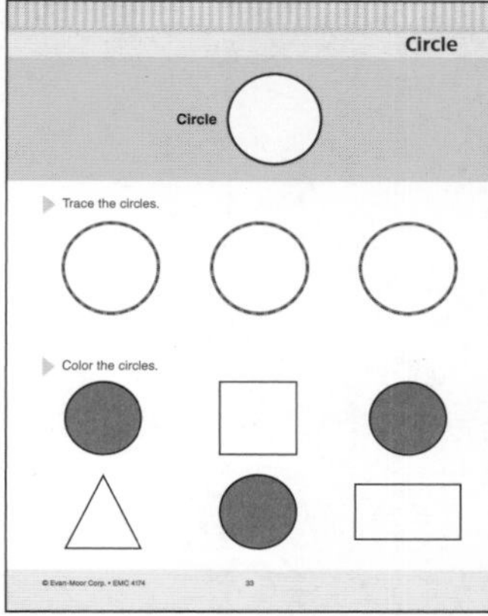

Page 34

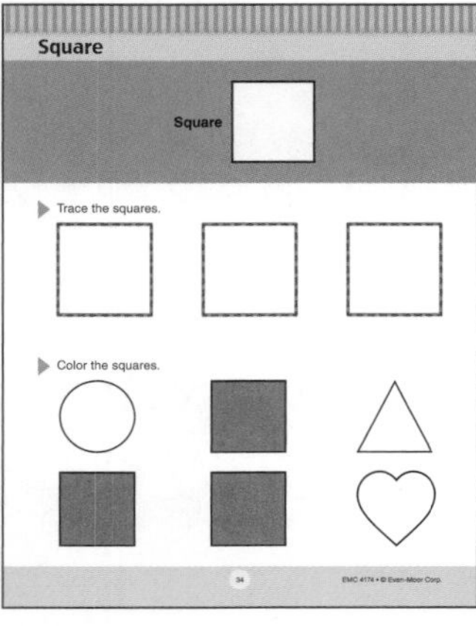

Page 35

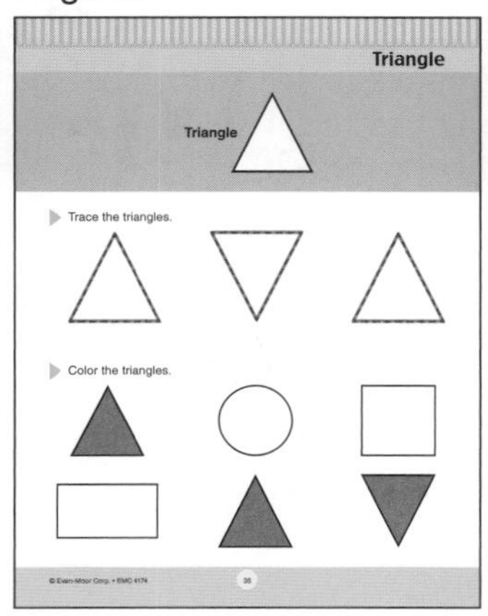

Page 36

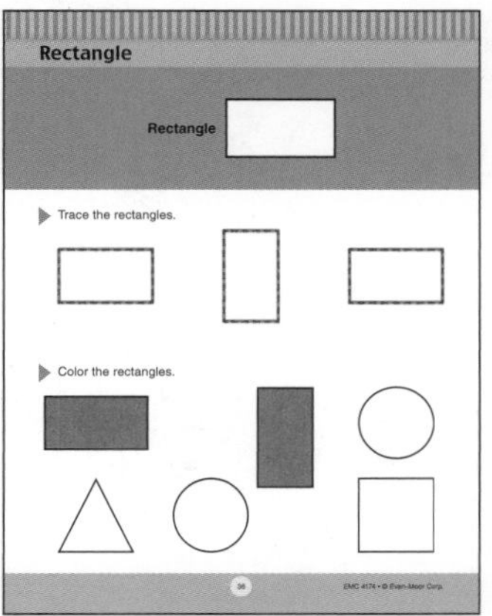

Page 37

Page 38

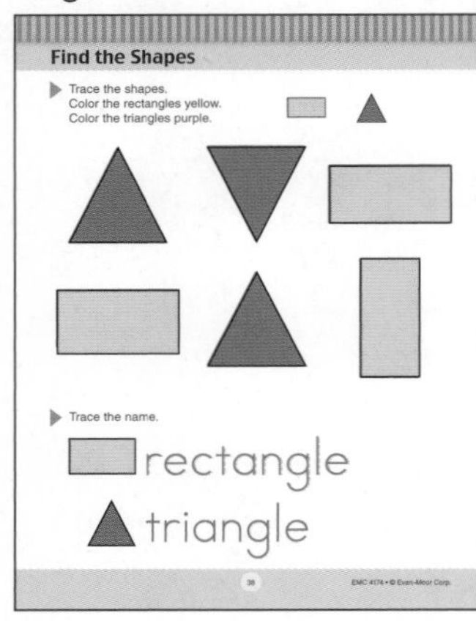

Page 39

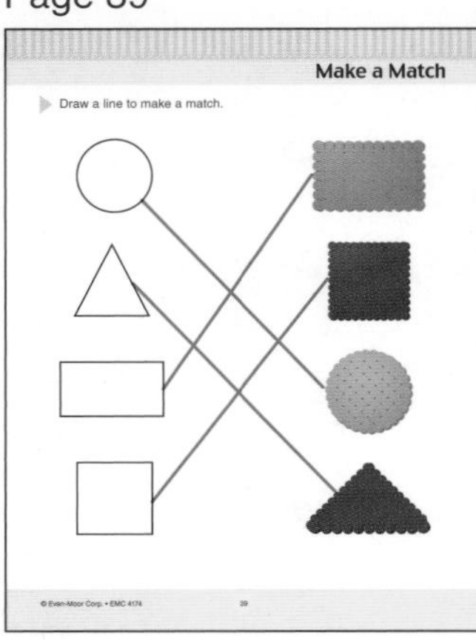

Page 40

Page 41

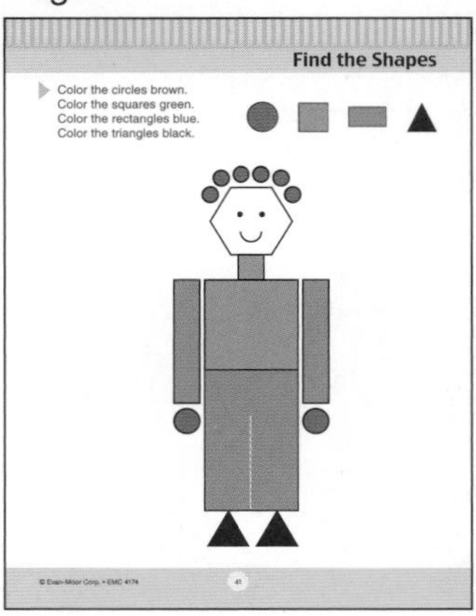

Page 42

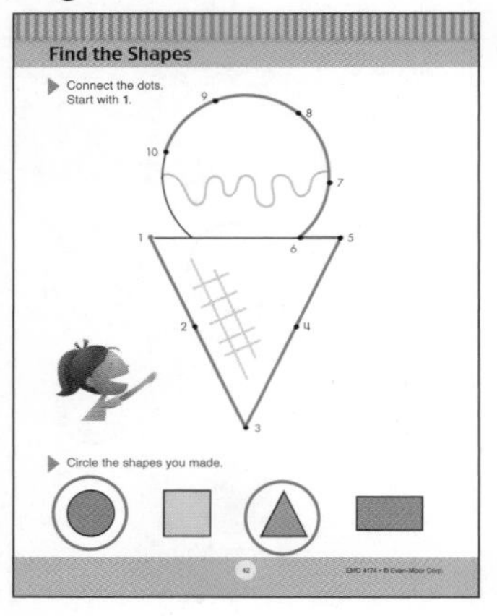

Page 43

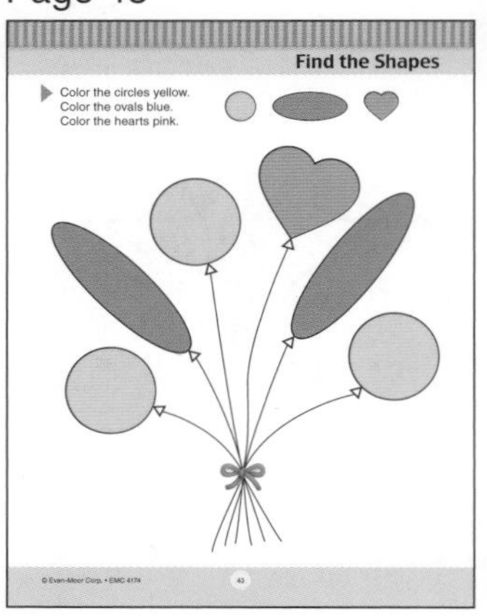

Page 44

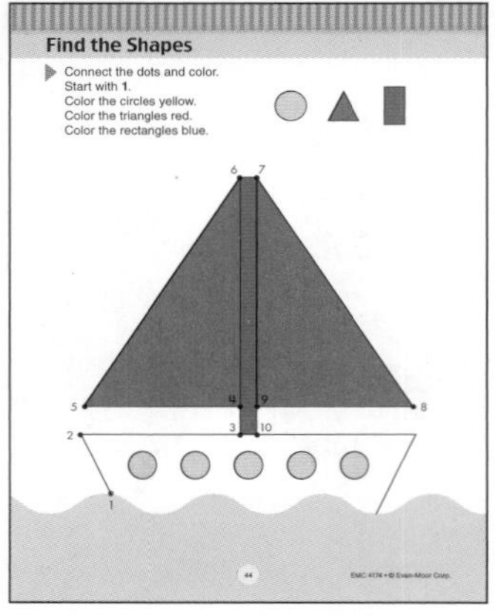

Page 45

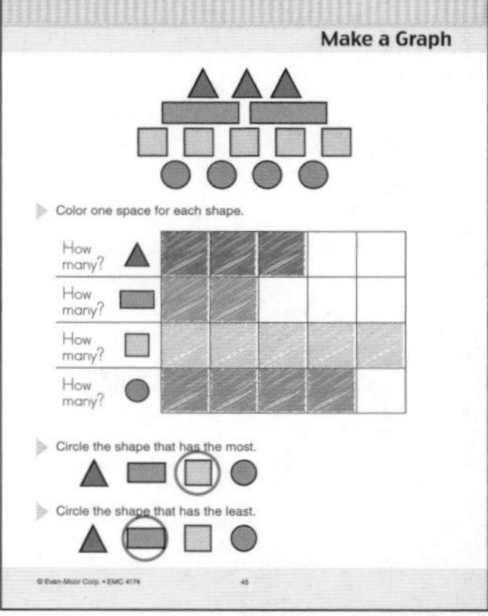

Page 46

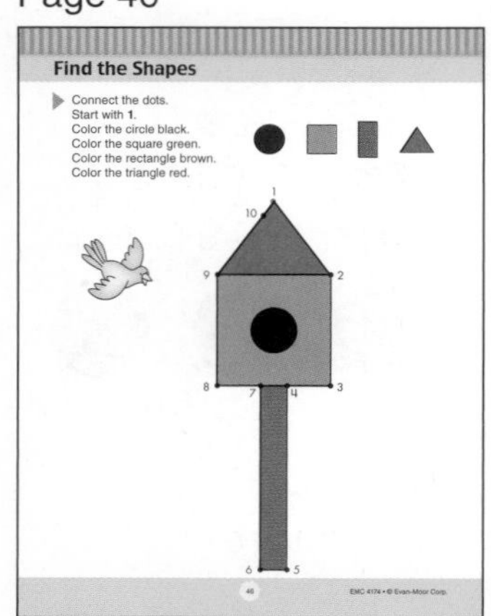

Page 47

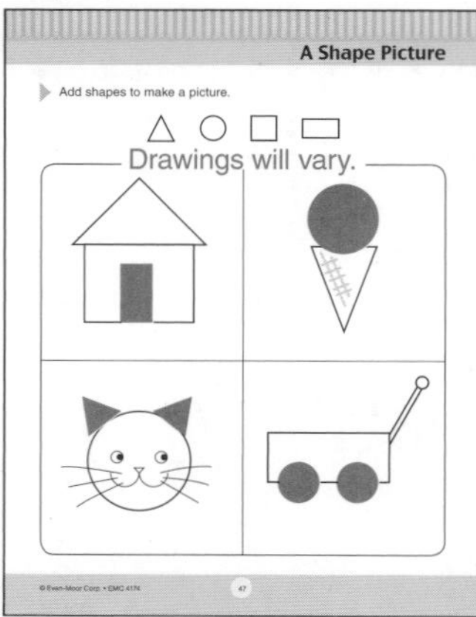

Page 48

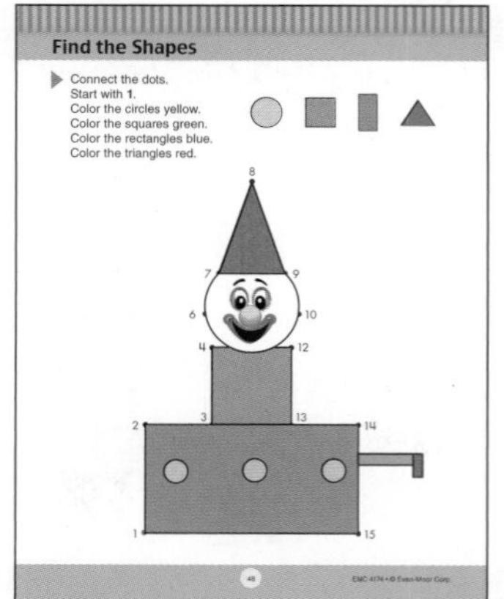

Page 49

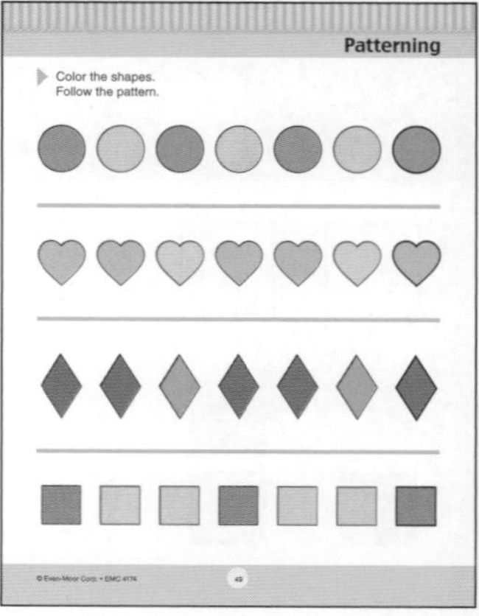

Page 50

Page 51

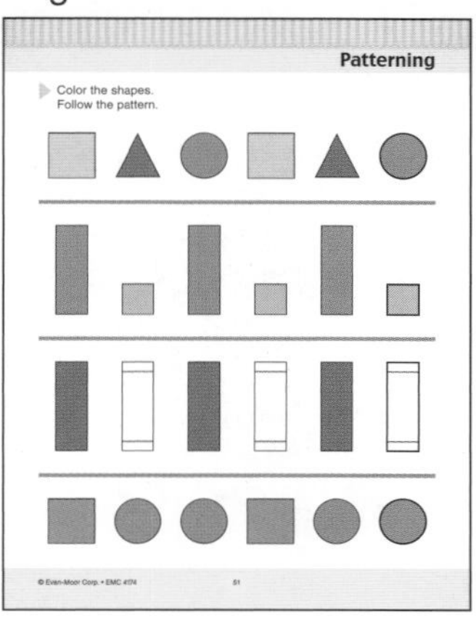

Page 52

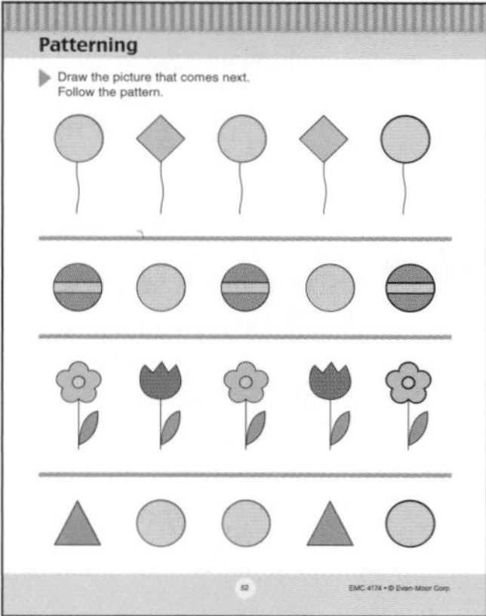

Page 53

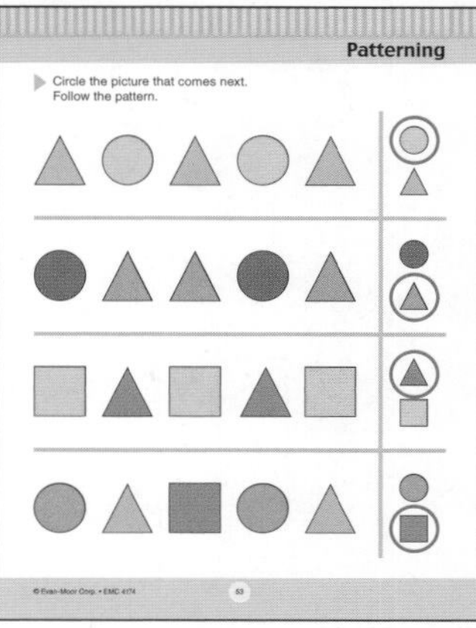

Page 54

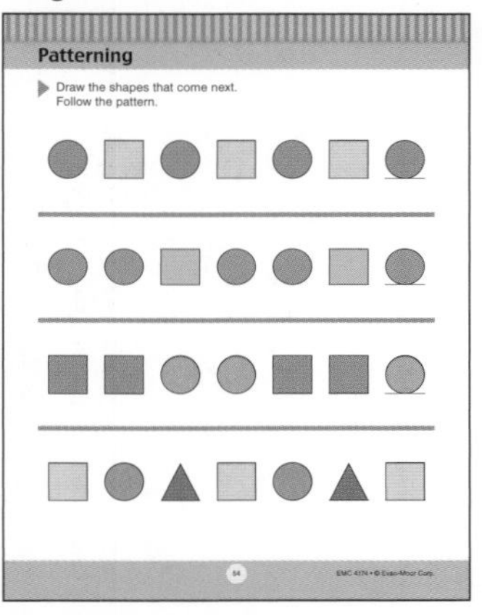

Page 55

Page 56

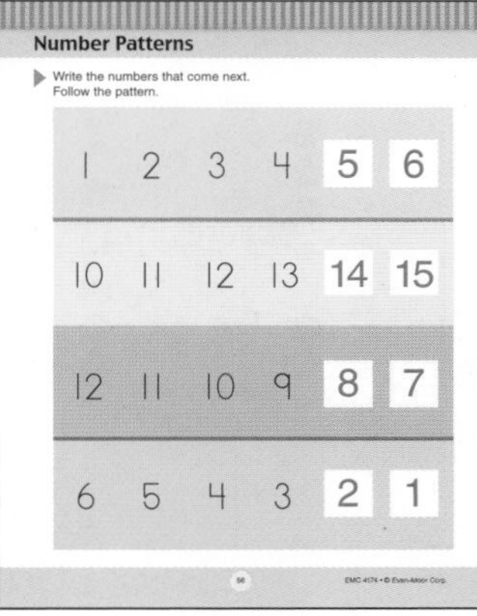

Page 57

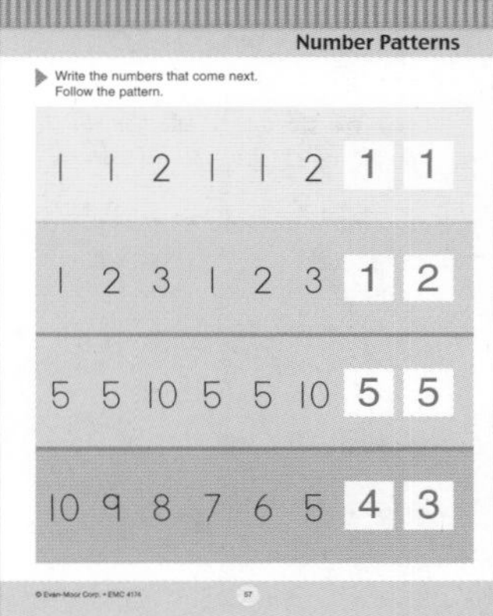

Page 58

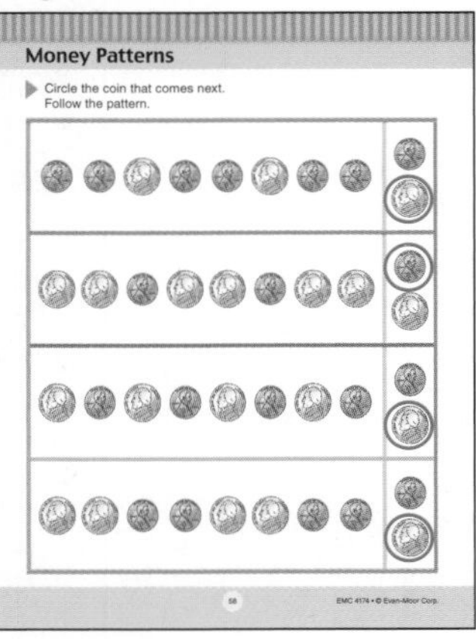

Page 59

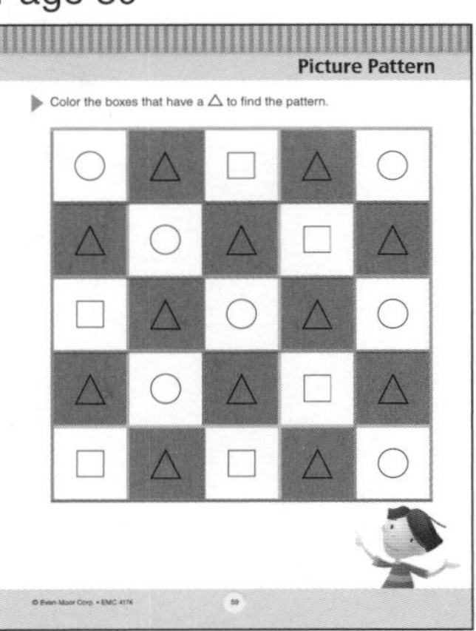

Page 60

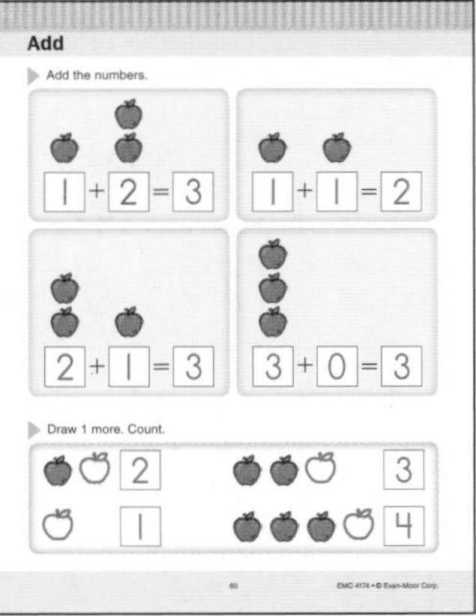

Page 61

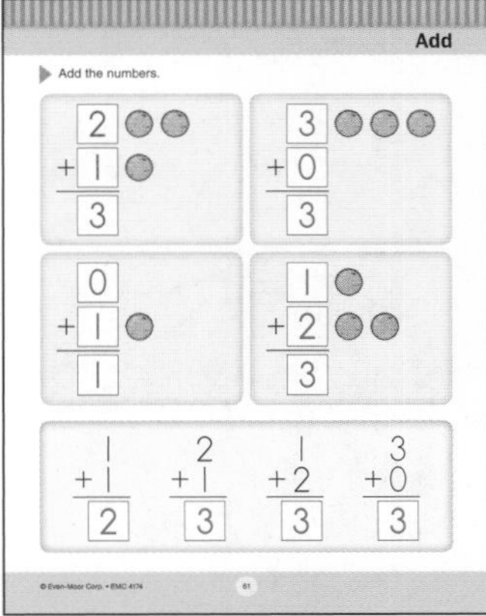

Page 62

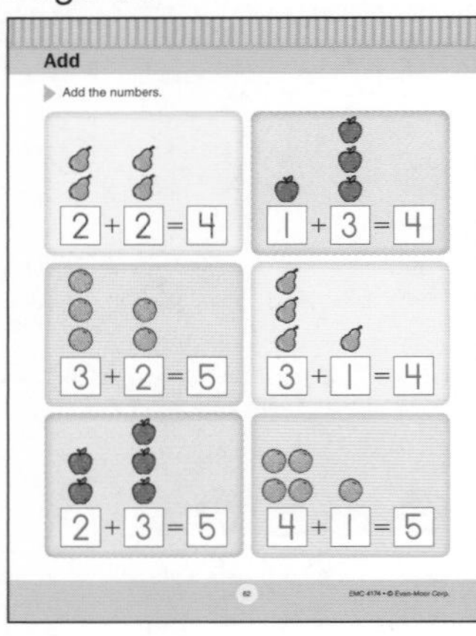

Page 63

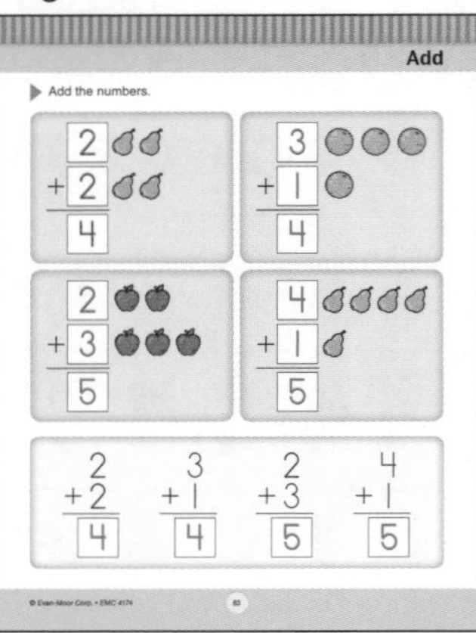

Page 64

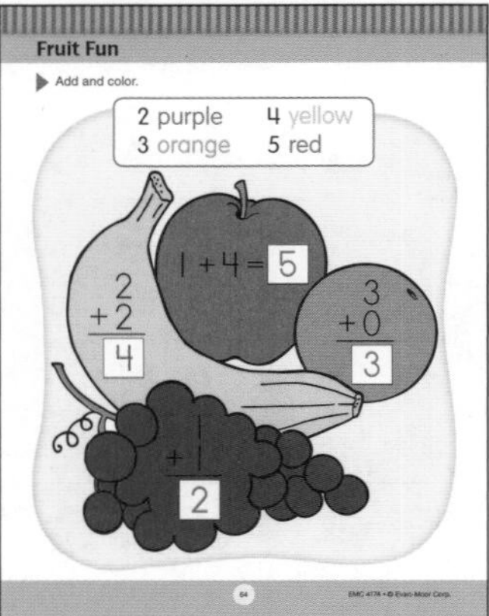

Page 65

Page 66

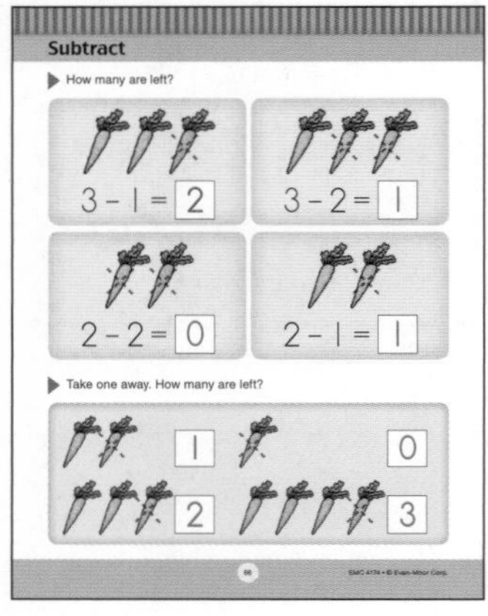

Page 67

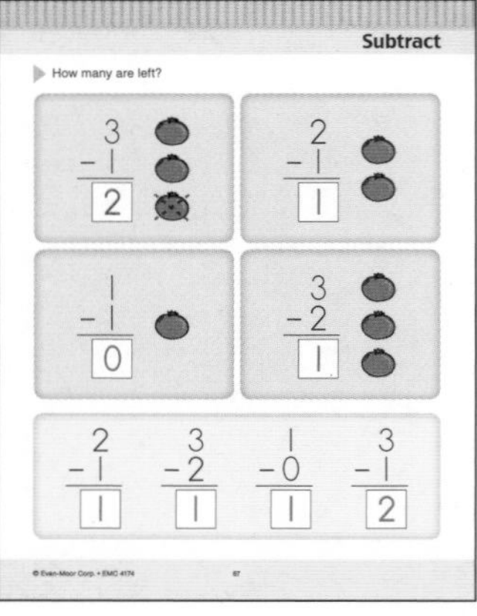

Page 68

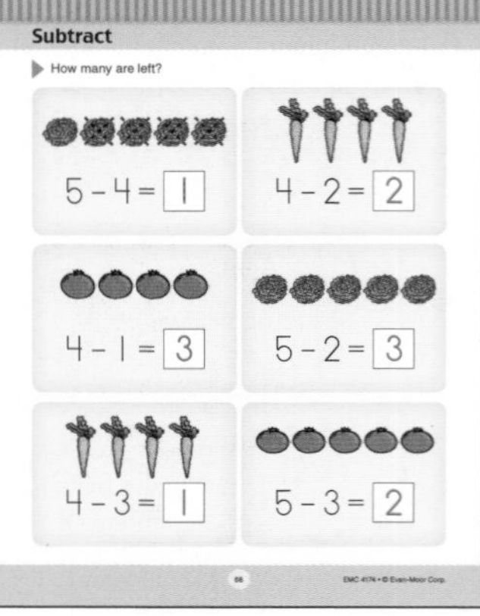

Page 69

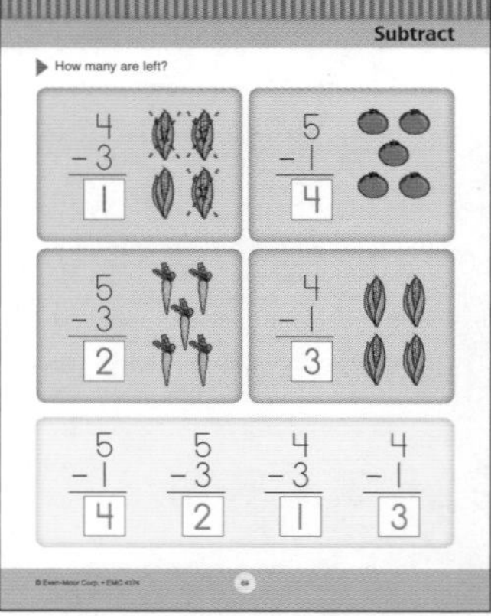

Page 70

Page 71

Page 72

Page 73

Page 74

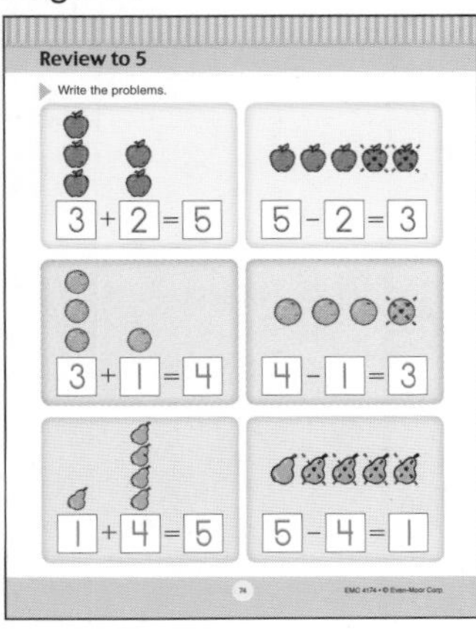
Review to 5

Write the problems.

3 + 2 = 5 | 5 − 2 = 3
3 + 1 = 4 | 4 − 1 = 3
1 + 4 = 5 | 5 − 4 = 1

Page 75

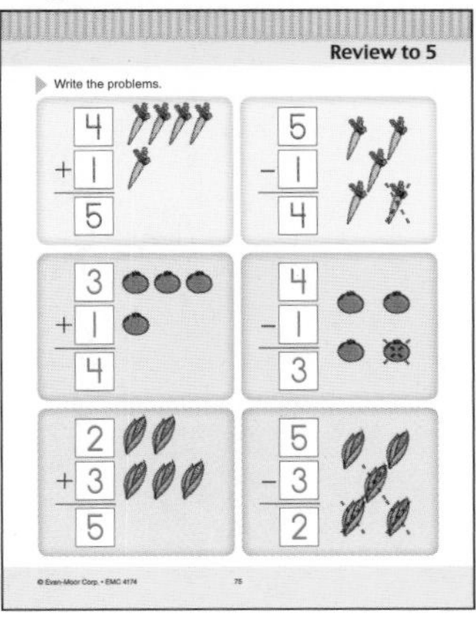
Review to 5

Write the problems.

4 + 1 = 5 | 5 − 1 = 4
3 + 1 = 4 | 4 − 1 = 3
2 + 3 = 5 | 5 − 3 = 2

Page 76

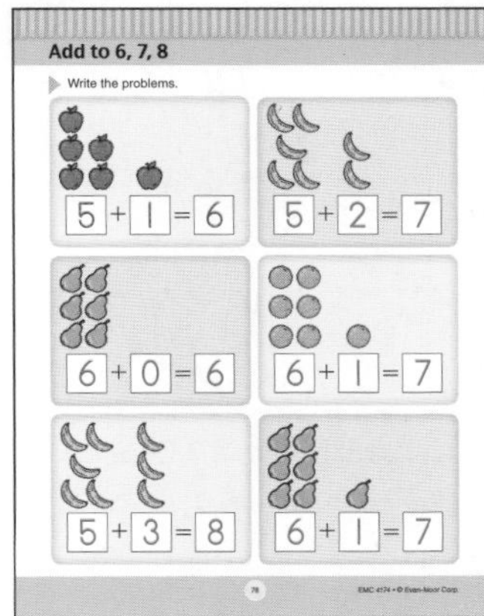
Add to 6, 7, 8

Write the problems.

5 + 1 = 6 | 5 + 2 = 7
6 + 0 = 6 | 6 + 1 = 7
5 + 3 = 8 | 6 + 1 = 7

Page 77

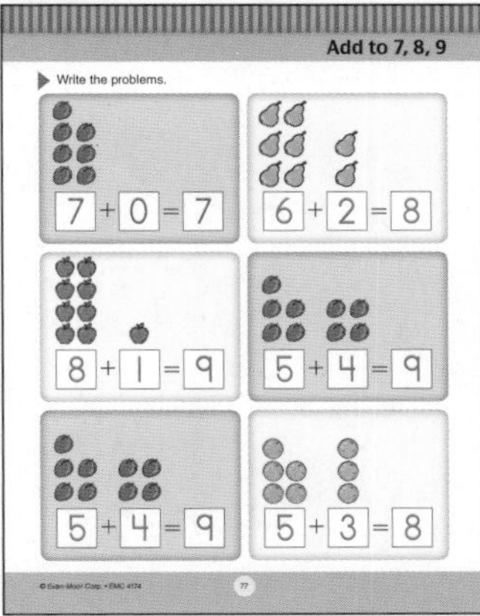
Add to 7, 8, 9

Write the problems.

7 + 0 = 7 | 6 + 2 = 8
8 + 1 = 9 | 5 + 4 = 9
5 + 4 = 9 | 5 + 3 = 8

Page 78

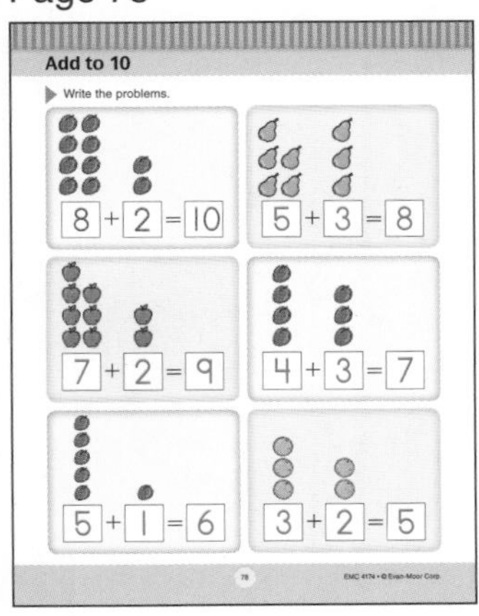
Add to 10

Write the problems.

8 + 2 = 10 | 5 + 3 = 8
7 + 2 = 9 | 4 + 3 = 7
5 + 1 = 6 | 3 + 2 = 5

Page 79

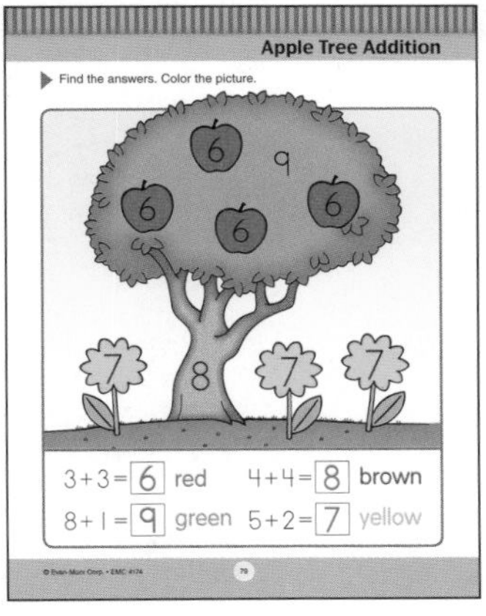
Apple Tree Addition

Find the answers. Color the picture.

3 + 3 = 6 red | 4 + 4 = 8 brown
8 + 1 = 9 green | 5 + 2 = 7 yellow

Page 80

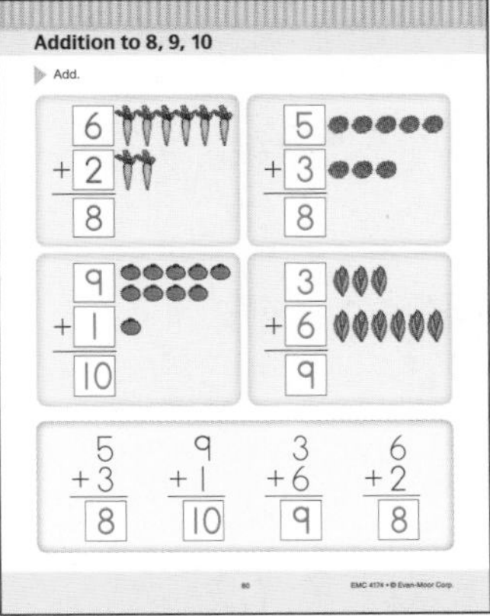
Addition to 8, 9, 10

Add.

6 + 2 = 8 | 5 + 3 = 8
9 + 1 = 10 | 3 + 6 = 9

5 + 3 = 8 | 9 + 1 = 10 | 3 + 6 = 9 | 6 + 2 = 8

Page 81

Picking Veggies

Add. Connect the dots. Start with 1.

3 + 6 = 9
8 + 0 = 8
4 + 3 = 7
3 + 3 = 6
4 + 1 = 5
2 + 2 = 4
0 + 3 = 3
1 + 1 = 2
1 + 0 = 1

Page 82

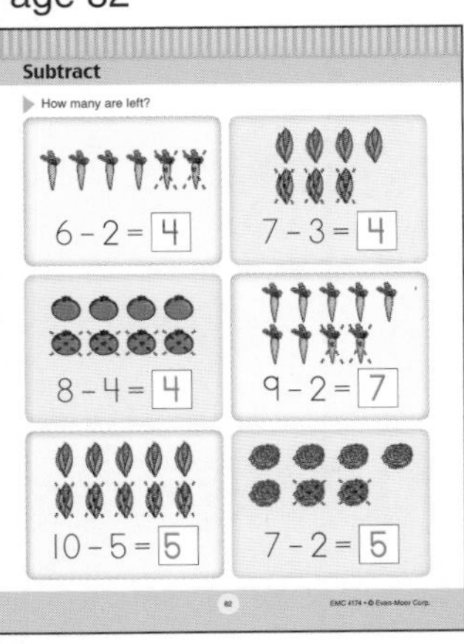
Subtract

How many are left?

6 − 2 = 4 | 7 − 3 = 4
8 − 4 = 4 | 9 − 2 = 7
10 − 5 = 5 | 7 − 2 = 5

Page 83

Funny Monkey

Find the answers. Color the picture.

6 − 3 = 3 brown | 7 − 0 = 7 orange
8 − 2 = 6 red | 10 − 5 = 5 yellow

Page 84

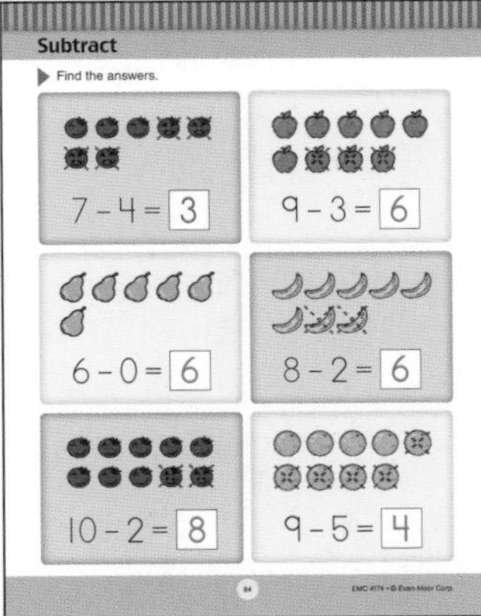
Subtract

Find the answers.

7 − 4 = 3 | 9 − 3 = 6
6 − 0 = 6 | 8 − 2 = 6
10 − 2 = 8 | 9 − 5 = 4

Page 85

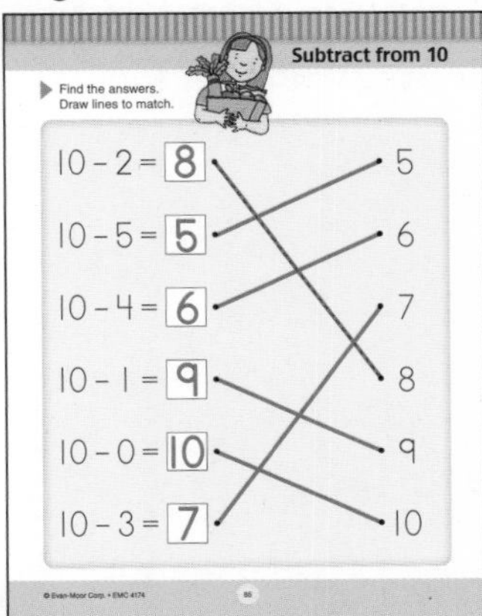
Subtract from 10

Find the answers. Draw lines to match.

10 − 2 = 8 | 5
10 − 5 = 5 | 6
10 − 4 = 6 | 7
10 − 1 = 9 | 8
10 − 0 = 10 | 9
10 − 3 = 7 | 10

Page 86

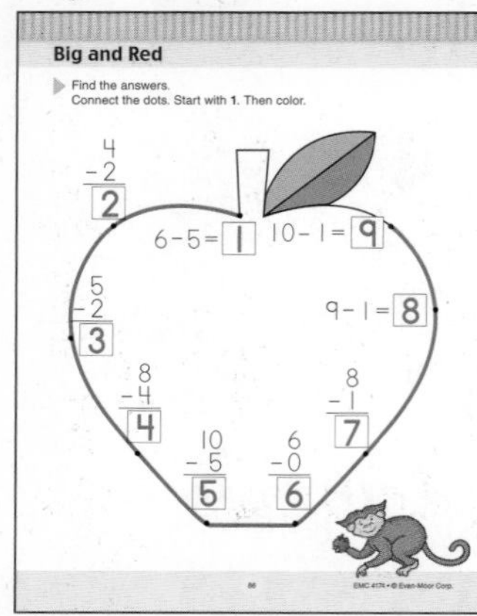

Page 87

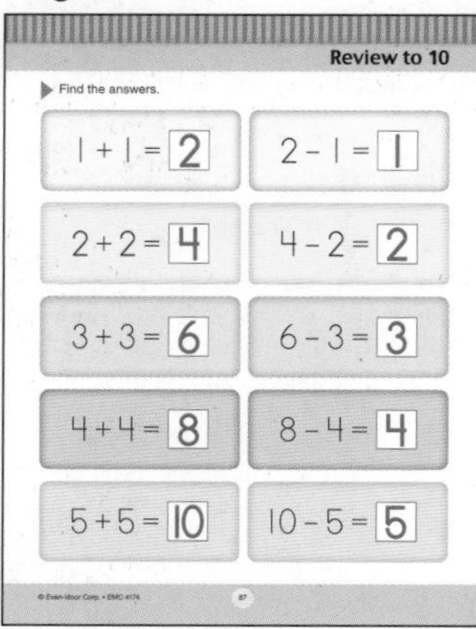

Page 88

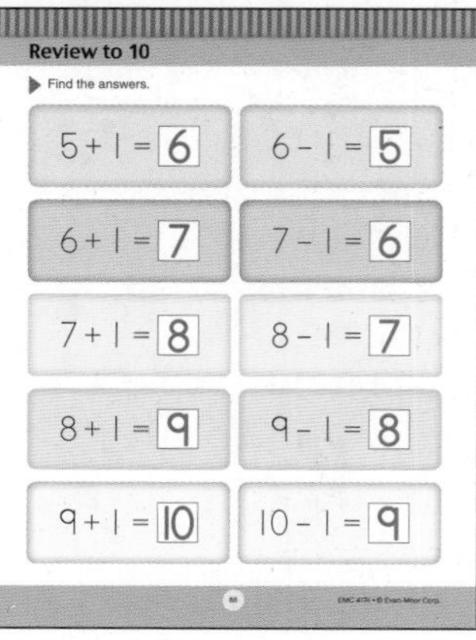